T0328604

Cambridge Elements

Elements in Bioethics and Neuroethics
edited by
Thomasine Kushner
California Pacific Medical Center, San Francisco

CONSCIENTIOUS OBJECTION IN MEDICINE

Mark Wicclair
University of Pittsburgh

CAMBRIDGE
UNIVERSITY PRESS

Shaftesbury Road, Cambridge CB2 8EA, United Kingdom

One Liberty Plaza, 20th Floor, New York, NY 10006, USA

477 Williamstown Road, Port Melbourne, VIC 3207, Australia

314–321, 3rd Floor, Plot 3, Splendor Forum, Jasola District Centre,
New Delhi – 110025, India

103 Penang Road, #05–06/07, Visioncrest Commercial, Singapore 238467

Cambridge University Press is part of Cambridge University Press & Assessment,
a department of the University of Cambridge.

We share the University's mission to contribute to society through the pursuit of
education, learning and research at the highest international levels of excellence.

www.cambridge.org
Information on this title: www.cambridge.org/9781009533584

DOI: 10.1017/9781009076081

First published 2024

A catalogue record for this publication is available from the British Library.

ISBN 978-1-009-53358-4 Hardback
ISBN 978-1-009-07479-7 Paperback
ISSN 2752-3934 (online)
ISSN 2752-3926 (print)

Cambridge University Press & Assessment has no responsibility for the persistence
or accuracy of URLs for external or third-party internet websites referred to in this
publication and does not guarantee that any content on such websites is, or will
remain, accurate or appropriate.

Conscientious Objection in Medicine

Elements in Bioethics and Neuroethics

DOI: 10.1017/9781009076081
First published online: March 2024

Mark Wicclair
University of Pittsburgh
Author for correspondence: Mark Wicclair, wicclair@pitt.edu

Abstract: The Element examines ethical and conceptual issues about conscientious objection in medicine. Concepts analyzed include conscientious objection, conscientious provision, conscience, moral complicity, and moral integrity. Several ongoing ethical controversies are identified and critically analyzed. One is a disagreement about whether conscientious objection is compatible with physicians' professional obligations. The Element argues that incompatibilists fail to offer a justifiable specification of professional obligations that supports their position. The Element also argues that a challenge for compatibilists who support a reason-giving requirement is to specify justifiable and unambiguous criteria for reviewing objectors' reasons. Arguments for and against requirements to inform and refer patients are critically analyzed, and an alternative, context-dependent requirement is offered. Another subject of controversy is about the justifiability of asymmetry between responses to conscientious objectors and conscientious providers. Typically, only the former receive accommodation. The Element critically examines arguments for asymmetry and maintains that none provides a convincing justification.

Keywords: conscientious objection, conscience, professional obligations, moral integrity, moral complicity

ISBNs: 9781009533584 (HB), 9781009074797 (PB), 9781009076081 (OC)
ISSNs: 2752-3934 (online), 2752-3926 (print)

Contents

1 Introduction

Conscientious objection to military service has a long history.[1] By contrast, conscientious objection in medicine is a relatively recent phenomenon. It became widespread when abortion services were decriminalized. The connection between the legalization or decriminalization of abortion and conscientious objection applies to developed countries – those in the "Global North" – as well to developing countries – those in the "Global South."[2] However, the focus of this discussion of the growth of conscientious objection in medicine will be on two representative countries in the former category – the United States and the United Kingdom.

In the United States, after the 1973 *Roe* v. *Wade* Supreme Court decision established a constitutional right to abortion, many obstetrician–gynecologists (OB–GYNs) who were morally and/or religiously opposed to pregnancy termination conscientiously objected. In the same year, the US Congress passed the Church Amendment (42 U.S.C. § 300a–7[b]), the first health-care "conscience clause" (legislation that protects health-care professionals who refuse to provide a good or service for ethical or religious reasons). The Church Amendment stated that receipt of funds under three federal programs did not authorize any court, public official, or "other public authority" to require individuals or institutions with ethical or religious objections to provide or assist in the provision of abortions or sterilizations (42 U.S.C. § 300a–7[b]).

In the United Kingdom, a legislative act, the Abortion Act of 1967 (1967 c. 87), legalized abortion. Anticipating ethical or religious objections to performing abortions, a conscience clause was incorporated directly into the legislation. It included the following provision: "[N]o person shall be under any duty, whether by contract or by any statutory or other legal requirement, to participate in any treatment authorised by this Act to which he has a conscientious objection." However, objectors were not released from a "duty to participate in treatment which is necessary to save the life or to prevent grave permanent injury to the physical or mental health of a pregnant woman."

Advances in life-sustaining medical treatment also contributed to an increase in the scope and frequency of conscientious objection. During the second half of the twentieth century, the ability to prolong the lives of patients increased substantially. Some physicians believed that if it is medically possible to prolong a patient's life, they have an ethical and professional obligation to do so, and they conscientiously objected to forgoing life-sustaining treatment – either all measures, or specific measures such as medically provided nutrition and hydration (MPNH).

The scope of conscientious objection has expanded significantly beyond abortion, sterilization, and forgoing life-sustaining treatment. Its scope related to reproductive health includes contraception and fertility treatments. Its scope related to death and dying includes donation after circulatory determination of death (DCDD), palliative sedation to unconsciousness, and medical assistance in dying (MAID). And its scope is not limited to reproductive health care and death and dying.

Undoubtedly, conscientious objection in medicine – and health care generally – has quickly grown from a relatively limited phenomenon to one that encompasses a broad range of medical services. Corresponding to the increase in its scope and incidence, it has generated a substantial scholarly literature. This Element provides a critical analysis of key positions and debates about ethical and conceptual issues within that scholarly literature.

2 What Is Conscientious Objection?

One obvious answer would be to define conscientious objection as an objection that is conscience-based – that is, based on an individual's conscience. However, since there are several different conceptions of conscience,[3] this is not an unambiguous answer. According to one familiar conception, conscience is a mental faculty that has the dual function of making moral judgments and guiding behavior.[4] This conception maintains that people consult or exercise their conscience to determine whether their past or contemplated future actions or omissions are morally wrong. A religious conception maintains that "conscience may be understood as enabling moral agents to know whether an act conforms to the divine law, that is, to God's standard of right and wrong."[5]

Broader conceptions identify conscience with practical reason, moral agency, or capacity for moral choice. Practical reason is associated with a common conception of conscience during the Middle Ages,[6] and the conception of conscience as moral agency or capacity for moral choice is associated with later followers of Stoicism.[7]

Some conceptions reject the view that a function of conscience is to make moral judgments. A classic example is Kant's conception of conscience as an "inner court."[8] According to Kant, it is not the function of a person's conscience to make moral judgments (e.g., to ascertain their duties). Such ethical judgments are a function of moral reasoning (practical reason). The exercise of conscience involves a process of self-reflection which has the aim of determining whether a person's past or contemplated actions are consistent with duties ascertainable by practical reasoning. Metaphorically, this determination takes place within an inner court, in which the agent acts as prosecutor, defense attorney, and judge. A "guilty" verdict reflects a finding that the agent's past or contemplated actions are not consistent with duties ascertained by practical reasoning. Kant refers to conscience as an "instinct" and claims that agents cannot escape from their conscience or its inner voice.[9]

A more recent conception that does not attribute to conscience the function of making moral judgments maintains instead that its primary function is as a sort of liaison between a person's ethical convictions and actions.[10] According to this conception, conscience promotes conformity between ethical belief and action. It "follows rather than authorizes moral judgments."[11]

Some contemporary scholars explicitly reject the conception of conscience as a mental faculty with an epistemic function.[12] One conception identifies it with the Freudian "superego," which is a means to protect society from the natural (innate) aggression of its members: "Civilization ... obtains mastery over the individual's dangerous desire for aggression by weakening and disarming it and by setting up an agency within him to watch over it, like a garrison in a conquered city."[13] A key feature of the superego is the internalization of previously external standards. Freud maintains that prior to the development of the superego, individuals cannot be said to have a conscience or experience feelings of guilt.

A contemporary, expansive conception of conscience identifies it as "the faculty in human beings with which they search for life's ultimate meaning."[14] According to this conception, conscience is "that seat of imagination, emotion, thought, and will through which each person seeks meaning in his or her own way."[15]

To define conscientious objection in medicine, one need not specify and justify a conception of conscience. Conscientious objections can be understood as objections that are based on a physician's *moral convictions*. This is a common understanding of the concept. Physicians can object to a medical service for a variety of reasons. Objections can be characterized as conscientious objections if and only if they are based on a physician's moral convictions. The crucial question is whether the reason for objecting is the belief that an act (or omission) is morally wrong. It does not matter whether the objection is *conscience*-based in any sense other than whether it is based on the physician's *moral convictions*.

Physicians' moral convictions can be based on their religious beliefs; or they can have a nonreligious basis. The relevant moral convictions can be about the obligations of the individual *as a moral agent*, and they can involve beliefs about the obligations of the individual *as a member of the medical profession*. In the latter case, the objection is based on the *physician's conception* of the goals of medicine and the professional obligations of physicians. For example, an OB–GYN refuses to perform abortions unless they are required to prevent the imminent death of pregnant women because – contrary to the established view within the profession – the OB–GY believes that unless this condition is satisfied, terminating pregnancies is incompatible with a physician's obligation to promote health.

2.1 Moral Complicity

When physicians conscientiously object to a medical service, they sometimes object only to providing the service. For example, an OB–GYN who conscientiously objects to abortion refuses to perform pregnancy terminations but is willing to refer patients to abortion providers. However, conscientious objections can go beyond refusing to provide medical services. Physicians can also conscientiously object to informing patients about a medical service or referring patients to a health professional who is willing to provide the service. For example, an emergency room physician who conscientiously objects to emergency contraception (EC) might refuse to provide it to rape victims who request it and also refuse to inform them of the availability of medication that can prevent pregnancy even several days after intercourse. More broadly, physicians can conscientiously object to *any perceived participation* in a medical service that is contrary to their moral convictions. For example, a physician who conscientiously objects to gender reassignment surgery might refuse to treat a patient who experiences post–gender reassignment surgery complications. Claims of conscientious objection that go beyond objections to providing a medical service are generally based on the provider's interest in avoiding moral complicity and the belief that direct or indirect participation in an immoral practice can involve moral complicity.

Michael Bayles offers a complicity-based reason for OB–GYNs who conscientiously object to abortion to refuse to refer to willing providers:

> If a physician sincerely believes abortion in a particular case is morally wrong, he cannot consistently advise a patient where she may obtain one. To do so would be to assist someone in immoral conduct by knowingly providing a means to it. The physician would bear some responsibility for the wrongful deed. Believing the abortion to be morally wrong, he believes that it is wrong for anyone to perform it and for the woman to obtain it. If he directs her to a physician who will perform it, then he assists both of them in acting wrongfully.[16]

In response, some bioethicists distinguish between direct and indirect referral and maintain that complicity is absent when referral is indirect. According to Frank Chervenak and Laurence McCullough, direct referral is said to involve communication between physicians – one who refers and one who receives the referral.[17] The former contacts the latter and takes steps to assure that the patient will receive a medically indicated service that the former is unable or unwilling to provide. By contrast, indirect referrals are limited to providing patients with information (e.g., the names and contact information of providers from whom they can receive the service at issue).

Chervenak and McCullough maintain that although it might be plausible to ascribe moral complicity in cases of direct referral, a physician who provides an indirect referral "cannot reasonably be understood to be a party to, or complicit in, a subsequent decision that is the sole province of the patient's subsequent exercise of autonomy in consultation with a referral physician."[18]

Karen Brauer, a past president of Pharmacists for Life, challenges the claim that indirect referrals do not establish complicity: "That's like saying, 'I don't kill people myself but let me tell you about the guy down the street who does.' What's that saying? 'I will not off your husband, but I know a buddy who will?' It's the same thing."[19] Giving the wife information that will enable her to enlist the services of a willing killer satisfies the criteria of "indirect referral." Arguably, if the "referral" results in the spouse's murder, the person who provided the information cannot avoid complicity by claiming that the decision to kill "is the sole province of the ... [wife's] subsequent exercise of autonomy in consultation with a referral [killer]." Accordingly, characterizing a referral as indirect may not suffice to establish a lack of moral complicity, and additional factors may need to be considered.

Drawing on the natural law tradition, Daniel Sulmasy offers a complex multifactor account of moral complicity.[20] He identifies several conditions. One, "formal cooperation," is a sufficient condition of moral complicity. According to this condition, if x shares in the intent (i.e., goal or purpose) of a wrongdoer y, x is morally complicit in y's wrongdoing. Accordingly, if a physician who has a conscience-based objection to palliative sedation to unconsciousness refers a patient who requests it to another physician with the intent of helping the patient achieve their goal, the physician is morally complicit in a perceived wrongdoing. However, a physician who has a conscience-based objection to providing a requested good or service can provide a referral without sharing the patient's purpose. The physician can intend only to respect the patient's autonomy and/or to fulfill a perceived professional obligation to refer. A similar point applies to disclosing options, including those that a physician is unwilling to provide due to conscience-based objections.

According to Sulmasy, if formal cooperation is absent, it is necessary to assess "material cooperation," and he provides seven questions to guide an assessment of moral complicity:

(1) How necessary is one's cooperation to the carrying out of the act? Could it occur without one's cooperation? The more likely that it could occur without one's cooperation, the more justified is one's cooperation. (2) How proximate is one to the act, in space and time and in the causal chain? The further removed one is, the more justified is one's cooperation. (3) Is one under any degree of duress to perform the act? Is someone compelling the act at

gunpoint? Does failure to cooperate mean loss of livelihood and ability to provide for a family? The more duress one is under, the more justifiable is one's cooperation. (4) How likely is one's cooperation to become habitual? The less likely, the more justifiable. (5) Is there a significant potential for scandal? I am using scandal here in the technical sense of leading others to believe that the one who is providing the material cooperation actually approves of the act so that observers might thereby be led to think it morally permissible. The less the potential for scandal, the more permissible the cooperation. (6) Does one have a special role that would be violated by this action? The less one has special role responsibilities that potentially would be contravened by the act, the more justifiable it is. (7) Does one have a proportionately important reason for the cooperation? That is, is there some morally important good that will come about because of one's indirect cooperation? If so, one has a better justification for cooperation.[21]

According to these criteria, moral complicity is a matter of degree.

There are other conceptions of moral complicity, and there is ongoing controversy among their defenders and detractors. It is beyond the scope of this Element to engage further in the debate, much less to identify and defend a justifiable conception. Fortunately, that is unnecessary. If, as maintained in Section 3, a key aim of accommodation is to give physicians moral space in which to practice medicine in accordance with their moral beliefs, considerable deference should be given to a physician's conception of moral complicity. Granted, beliefs about complicity are second-order metaethical beliefs, but they can shape first-order normative ethical beliefs.

2.2 Some Important Distinctions

It may be understandable that physicians who believe that a medical service is morally wrong would want to prevent patients from acting immorally. However, conscientious objection should not be confused with obstruction. The aim of conscientious objection is for physicians to avoid providing – or participation in the provision of – medical services that violate their moral convictions. Metaphorically, it is to keep their hands "morally clean." In this respect, conscientious objection is "inner-directed." By contrast, obstruction is "outer-directed." The aim is to prevent others from actions that the physician believes are morally wrong.

Civil disobedience is another type of outer-directed action that should be distinguished from conscientious objection. Whereas conscientious objection typically is inner-directed with the aim of avoiding acting against one's conscience, civil disobedience is public and outer-directed.[22] An aim of civil disobedience is to promote change – typically through unlawful but peaceful protests – by calling attention to unjust laws and policies and increasing pressure for change. Whereas individuals who engage in acts of civil disobedience can expect penalties for unlawful acts, conscientious objectors seek exemptions that will protect them from penalties for refusing to provide specific medical services.[23]

Conscientious *objection* involves a *refusal* to provide legally and institutionally permitted medical services that are contrary to a physician's moral convictions. By contrast, what some call conscientious *provision*[24] and others call conscientious *commitment*[25] occurs when physicians (conscientious providers) offer legally or institutionally prohibited medical services because they believe that they have a moral and/or professional obligation to offer them. In the United States, several states have enacted legislation that prohibits gender-affirming care for adolescents.[26] These laws have triggered instances of conscientious provision. Some pediatricians who practice in states that prohibit gender-affirming care for adolescents have continued to offer it when they believe it is necessary to protect and promote the health and well-being of their patients. Restrictions on abortion have also triggered conscientious provision. In the United States, occasions for abortion-related conscientious provision are likely to increase in the aftermath of *Dobbs* v. *Jackson Women's Health Organization* (142 S. Ct. 2228) – the US Supreme Court decision that overturned *Roe* v. *Wade*. As result of *Dobbs*, states are now legally permitted to prohibit or substantially restrict abortion, and several have done so.[27] Ironically, overturning the decision that contributed to the extension of conscientious *objection* into the domain of health care may well act as a catalyst for conscientious *provision*.

Most of the focus of this Element will be on conscientious objection and conscientious objectors. However, asymmetry in accommodating conscientious objectors and conscientious providers will be examined in Section 5.

3 Should Conscientious Objectors Be Accommodated?

A general aim of accommodation is to give objecting physicians moral space in which to practice medicine consistent with their moral convictions. To ask whether physicians who conscientiously object should be accommodated is to ask whether they should be able to refuse to offer or provide medical services that are contrary to their moral convictions without facing sanctions or penalties, such as suspension, dismissal, loss of hospital privileges, censure, loss of medical license, or legal liability. It is generally agreed that physicians are free to refuse to offer or provide medical services that are illegal, contrary to standard of care, or outside the scope of their clinical competence. Consequently, the issue of accommodation generally does not arise for such refusals. However, with respect to medical services that are legal, standard of care, and within the scope of a physician's clinical competency, there is considerable controversy about whether or when to accommodate conscientious objectors.

3.1 Reasons to Accommodate

Defenders of conscientious objection offer one or more reasons to accommodate. They are *pro tanto* reasons for accommodation. That is, depending on the circumstances, there might be overriding reasons, such as the impact on patients and nonobjecting physicians, that justify not accommodating.

Moral integrity is among the most frequently cited reasons for accommodation – both by its defenders and its critics. Accommodation is said to provide objectors with moral space in which to practice medicine without compromising their moral integrity.[28]

3.1.1 Moral Integrity

There are several conceptions of moral integrity.[29] They include identity,[30] self-integration,[31] social,[32] objective,[33] reasonableness,[34] and intellectual virtue[35] conceptions. The identity conception will be used to explain what it means to maintain or undermine one's moral integrity and why maintaining it can matter to physicians.

According to the identity conception, persons have moral integrity only if they have a coherent set of core, self-defining moral beliefs. They are self-defining insofar as individuals associate them with their sense of who, or the kind of person, they are. Core moral beliefs are standards by which individuals judge themselves. Lynne McFall draws a useful distinction between *defeasible* and *identity-conferring* commitments.[36] The former can be "sacrificed without remorse" and without undermining one's integrity.[37] By contrast, the latter "reflect what we take to be the most important and so determine, to a large extent, our identities."[38] Core moral beliefs are identity-conferring commitments. Maintaining moral integrity requires consistently acting in accordance with one's core moral beliefs; and one's moral integrity is undermined or compromised if one acts contrary to them.

Defenders of conscientious objection have identified two respects in which maintaining moral integrity can matter to physicians.[39] First, it is claimed that moral integrity can be an essential component of their conception of a good or meaningful life. In this respect, moral integrity is said to have intrinsic worth or value to them. Second, it is claimed that a loss of moral integrity can be devastating because it can result in strong feelings of guilt, remorse, and shame as well as loss of self-respect.

Supporters of conscientious objection offer two additional reasons for enabling conscientious objectors to practice medicine without undermining their moral integrity. First, it is claimed that when withholding an exemption leads to a loss of moral integrity, the result can be a general decline in a person's moral character, which is particularly undesirable for physicians and other health-care professionals. Charles Hepler asserts a claim along these lines in relation to members of his profession (pharmacy): "We would be naive to expect a pharmacist to forsake his or her ethics in one area (e.g. abortion) while applying them for the patient's welfare in every other area."[40] Douglas White and Baruch Brody maintain that "if physicians do not have loyalty and fidelity to their own core moral beliefs, it is unrealistic to expect them to have loyalty and fidelity to their professional responsibilities."[41]

Second, it is claimed that moral integrity has intrinsic worth or value. Jeffrey Blustein maintains that integrity is "an important virtue of a certain sort, one that, when combined with other valuable traits, provides an additional ground for admiration of the individual."[42] The claim that moral integrity has intrinsic value has been challenged.[43] To be sure, it requires qualification. Insofar as moral integrity can involve a commitment to any ethical or religious belief, it does not guarantee ethically acceptable behavior. Depending on the content of a person's core moral beliefs, maintaining moral integrity can require invidious discrimination, genocide, cruelty, and so forth. Arguably, however, admiration and respect for moral integrity, like courage and honesty, is at least partially independent of an assessment of ends and consequences. That is, although we might justifiably withhold our admiration and respect if we judge the ends and consequences to be excessively bad, our admiration and respect is not always contingent on a favorable assessment of ends and consequences. Arguably, all other things being equal, the world is a better place if it includes people who are committed to principles and whose actions are not exclusively opportunistic or transactional.

Notably, to justify accommodation, objectors can appeal to an interest in maintaining their moral integrity – understood as the identity conception – only if providing the medical service to which they object is incompatible with their core moral convictions. Incompatibility with defeasible moral beliefs that do not implicate core moral beliefs is insufficient. Incompatibility with defeasible, noncore moral beliefs may cause moral distress, but not a loss of moral integrity. Although other conceptions of moral integrity do not have this specific requirement, they have some requirement(s) beyond incompatibility with one or more of an agent's moral beliefs. For example, Cheshire Calhoun's social conception requires interacting with others and engaging in a process of community deliberation;[44] Elizabeth Ashford's objective conception includes a constraint against the agent "being seriously deceived either about empirical facts or about the moral obligations she actually has";[45] and McFall's reasonableness conception limits beliefs to "ones a reasonable person might take to be of great importance and ones that a reasonable person might be tempted to sacrifice to some lesser yet still recognizable goods."[46] For many conceptions, requirements such as these are in addition to the identity conception's core moral belief condition.

Alberto Giubilini challenges the moral integrity justification. He claims that arguments in support of conscientious objection based on respect for the moral integrity of objectors are "extremely weak."[47] His critique is based on two claims: (1) Respect for moral integrity is not absolute – there are situations in which it cannot justify refusing to provide medical services. (2) There is no acceptable criterion for determining when it is justified to fail to respect the moral integrity of conscientious objectors. The second claim will be considered in Section 3.2. At this point, it suffices to note that Giubilini's critique is not inconsistent with the view that respect for moral integrity provides a *pro tanto* reason to accommodate. Indeed, his critique assumes that this is the case. If respecting moral integrity did not provide a *pro tanto* reason for accommodation, there would be no need to identify justified limitations.

Jeffrey Byrnes offers a challenge to the moral integrity justification that focuses on alleged insurmountable epistemological problems associated with core moral beliefs.[48] He claims that agents lack the "authentic self-knowledge" needed to reliably identify their core moral beliefs. In this respect, an agent's core moral beliefs are epistemically opaque to the agent; and, insofar as observers rely on the agent's self-knowledge, the agent's core moral beliefs are also epistemically opaque to them. As a result of this alleged epistemic opacity, Byrnes claims, "even if conscientious objection is permitted in health care, appeals to 'core moral beliefs' should not be the basis for such an objection."[49]

In response, it can be claimed that Byrnes assumes an unreasonably stringent standard of "authentic self-knowledge."[50] To be sure, moral agents do not have infallible self-knowledge. However, infallibility is an implausible requirement. It is sufficient that moral agents generally have a capacity to correctly identify their core moral beliefs. Moreover, the fact that moral agents sometimes can be mistaken about their core moral beliefs does not warrant a default assumption that it is more likely than not that moral agents cannot correctly identify them. Without relevant empirical data, a blanket policy of not recognizing conscientious objection based on core moral beliefs risks throwing out the baby with the bath water in two respects. First, a blanket refusal to consider objectors' core moral beliefs would inappropriately include health professionals who have legitimate grounds for accommodation. Second, even if agents are confused about whether some moral beliefs fall within the core or the periphery, there are likely to be actions that are so central to the core that their status is unquestionable. For both reasons, a blanket policy of not recognizing conscientious objection based on core moral beliefs would have a very high moral cost: some health professionals would not be given moral space in which to practice medicine without undermining their moral integrity.

To deny that moral agents generally have a capacity to reliably identify their core moral beliefs would have profound implications in health care beyond conscientious objection. For example, it would imply that it is mistaken to believe that patient decision-making can and should be informed by patients' deeply held values. If patients lack the requisite "authentic self-knowledge," it would be pointless to attempt to elicit their deeply held values in the process of shared decision-making or to ask them to consider those values when they execute advance directives. Suppose a decisionally capable patient with end-stage amyotrophic lateral sclerosis (ALS) refuses medically provided nutrition and hydration. When asked for their reason, they respond that dignity and independence are among their most important deeply held values. Arguably, it would be unjustified to disregard their decision solely on the grounds that patients generally lack authentic self-knowledge.

Notably, Byrnes identifies a preferable alternative to a blanket policy of discounting objections based on core moral beliefs: engaging in a dialogue with the agent. He cites the example of a medical student named Francesca who "has a well-identified set of core moral beliefs that are important to her self-understanding," which includes a commitment to social justice.[51] Consistent with this commitment, Francesca regularly volunteers at a food bank. When her volunteer work conflicts with her medical studies, Francesca is said to believe that "Med school is demanding too much of her and becoming a threat even to her self-identity."[52] Byrnes maintains that this is an example of a mistaken extension of an agent's core moral beliefs. However, according to him, that mistake is correctable by engaging in dialogue with Francesca: "And, I imagine that with time and through dialog she could be brought to see the commitment to visit the food pantry as [a] temporally limited commitment, and not constitutive of her identity like the underlying commitment to help the poor."[53] Later, he adds a general endorsement of dialogue: "A dialog, particularly a constructive and friendly one, opens the possibility that the agent could be corrected in her understanding of her core moral commitments."[54]

Obviously, dialogue cannot be expected to end disagreements between objectors and observers in all cases. For example, after an extended discussion with the department chair, an OB–GYN might continue to refuse any participation in abortion, including referral and counseling, and the department chair might continue to believe that the objector is mistakenly broadening the scope of their core moral beliefs. Who is right? The answer can depend in part on the objector's conception of moral complicity. Arguably, to assume that when observers conclude that a belief is defeasible, physicians must be mistaken if they consider it to be within the scope of their core moral beliefs begs the question and risks not giving due consideration to their moral integrity.

3.1.2 Additional Reasons to Accommodate

There are several additional reasons for accommodating conscientious objection. These are examined below.

Autonomy: Respect for autonomy can be cited as a reason to accommodate.[55] According to one conception, respect for autonomous agents is "to acknowledge their right to hold views, to make choices, and to take actions based on their values and beliefs."[56] On this conception it follows that refusing to accommodate physicians who believe that it is morally wrong to provide a requested medical service fails to respect their autonomy. Notably, however, the principle of respect for autonomy also applies to patients and not only to physicians.[57] Consequently, as in the case of other reasons for accommodation, respect for the autonomy of objectors can at most provide a *pro tanto* reason to accommodate. Depending on the circumstances, it may be justifiable, all things considered, to fail to respect objectors' autonomy.

Toleration: For some advocates of toleration, it is said to be a "first principle" in "post-industrial, democratic societies" which lack "any common moral ground" for "the adjudication of our differences."[58] Others provide a more positive defense of the principle. For example, Daniel Sulmasy cites "general principles of Lockean tolerance for a diversity of practices and persons in a flourishing, pluralistic, democratic society."[59] Either conception of tolerance can provide a reason to accommodate.

Epistemic humility or modesty: This is the view that although ethical beliefs can be correct or incorrect and justified or unjustified, we might be mistaken when we think that a particular ethical belief is correct or justified. This recognition suggests "modesty" or "humility" and a rejection of dogmatism in relation to beliefs that we do not accept.[60] It can be cited as a reason to accommodate.

Moral progress: Accommodation is said to preserve the medical profession's ability to "morally self-correct" and its capacity to be "reformable from within."[61] Outliers of today can be recognized as moral pioneers in the future. Past examples include physicians who objected to involuntary sterilization and withholding surgery to correct duodenal atresia in newborns with Down syndrome before those practices were widely condemned.

Quality of patient care: It is claimed that not receiving accommodation can negatively impact patient care.[62] Some claim physicians who are not accommodated can experience emotional or moral distress, which in turn can promote callousness and "divestiture."[63] The latter is said to occur "when the value of responding with care to others becomes less centrally and importantly constitutive of his personal and professional identity."[64] In addition, if physicians' unconventional beliefs are not tolerated, they might be less likely to be tolerant of patients' diverse backgrounds and beliefs.[65] Finally, it has been claimed that a "troubled conscience" can promote burnout.[66]

Diversity in the medical profession: It is claimed that accommodation promotes a diverse medical profession.[67] A policy of nonaccommodation can discourage people with diverse cultural, faith, and/or moral backgrounds from entering the profession.

Moral sensitivity: It is claimed that a failure to accommodate can affect the type of people who become physicians.[68] Telling people that, in effect, if they become doctors, they must leave their personal moral beliefs at the clinic door might discourage individuals who are ethically sensitive, compassionate, and empathetic from becoming physicians.

3.1.3 Can Physicians' Claims of Conscience Provide Pro Tanto *Reasons for Accommodation?*

Whereas defenders of conscientious objection maintain that one or more of the eight abovementioned reasons provide a *pro tanto* justification for accommodating conscientious objectors, Alberto Giubilini argues that claims of conscience do not provide a moral reason for accommodation.[69] Although he denies that claims of conscience can provide a justifying reason for refusing to provide medical services, he maintains that "sometimes there are good reasons to allow doctors to object to certain procedures that they would otherwise be socially or legally expected to perform."[70] However, these reasons are said to be acceptable only if they are based on the "values and principles of the medical profession" and not on physicians' personal moral beliefs.[71]

Giubilini supports his thesis with a *reductio ad absurdum* argument that requires us to consider two types of conscientious objections. One is a standard case of conscientious objection to abortion. The other is a fictional case of a physician who objects to administering antibiotics because they believe that bacteria have a significant moral status – the same moral status that anti-abortionists attribute to human fetuses. If we were to assume that claims of conscience provide a moral reason for accommodation, there would be a moral reason to accommodate physicians with conscience-based objections to abortion as well as antibiotics – presumably a conclusion that would strike defenders of accommodation as counterintuitive.

Giubilini goes on to consider possible overriding reasons in both cases. He identifies two types of overriding considerations. One is harm to patients and the other is inconsistency with core values and principles of contemporary (Western) medicine. With respect to harm, Giubilini argues that the same constraints on accommodation that protect patients when physicians object to abortion (e.g., referral and availability of physicians who can perform the procedure in a timely manner) can protect patients when doctors refuse to administer antibiotics. Therefore, protecting patients from harm cannot justify selectively not accommodating physicians who object to antibiotics.

Giubilini concedes that the values and principles of contemporary medicine can justify refusing to accommodate physicians who object to administering antibiotics. Indeed, it is the absurdity of a physician refusing to provide a basic, effective, and routine means to promote patient health and well-being that seems to underlie the intuition that conscience-based objections to administering antibiotics are unacceptable. A conscience-based objection to administering antibiotics is so clearly contrary to the principles and values of contemporary medicine that it is a special case in which critics of conscientious objection might well be justified to tell the physician to "choose another livelihood"[72] or to "select an area of medicine, such as radiology, that will not put them in situations that conflict with their personal morality or, if there is no such area, leave the profession."[73]

Giubilini claims, however, that the same overriding reason applies to abortion: "consistency with professional values does not seem to provide a valid criterion for distinguishing between the objection to abortion and the objection to antibiotics. This is because ... objection to abortion is not consistent with the values and principles of contemporary Western medicine."[74] He concludes that "the rights to the two types of objection [abortion and antibiotics] stand or fall together."[75] Presumably, this conclusion will also strike defenders of accommodation as counterintuitive. However, they can challenge an assumption in Giubilini's argument.

The assumption in question is that refusing to provide abortions and refusing to administer antibiotics are equally inconsistent with the principles and values of (Western) contemporary medicine. In the case of the physician who is morally opposed to administering antibiotics, there is an obvious, straightforward, and uncontroversial justification for denying an exemption: refusing to administer antibiotics when they are clinically indicated is inconsistent with core principles and values of contemporary medicine. Arguably, however, the core principles and values of contemporary medicine do not provide an equally obvious, straightforward, and uncontroversial justification for denying exemptions to physicians who are morally opposed to abortion. Whereas it is beyond doubt that administering antibiotics to treat bacterial infections is a core medical procedure in contemporary Western medicine, the same cannot be said about abortion. Whether abortion is consistent with, let alone required by, the goals of medicine is a question that involves complex and controversial normative and conceptual issues (e.g., the goals of medicine, the moral status of human fetuses, the scope of women's rights to control what happens in and to their bodies, and the concepts of health and disease).

However, even if Giubilini does not show that "the rights to the two types of objection [abortion and antibiotics] stand or fall together," the case of the physician who has a moral objection to administering antibiotics presents a challenge for supporters of conscientious objection. They appear to have two options in such cases: (1) They can maintain that claims of conscience provide a moral reason for granting exemptions, but there is a legitimate overriding reason when the physician's refusal is incompatible with core principles and values of contemporary (Western) medicine. (2) They can maintain that claims of conscience do not provide a moral reason for granting exemptions when the physician's refusal is incompatible with core principles and values of contemporary (Western) medicine. There is no practical difference between these two options. According to both, when refusals are incompatible with core principles and values of contemporary (Western) medicine, objectors should not be accommodated.

3.2 Objections to Conscientious Objection and Accommodation

A frequently voiced objection to accommodation draws upon an alleged difference between conscientious objection to performing compulsory military service and conscientious objection to providing specific medical services.[76] Unlike compulsory military service, it is claimed, becoming a physician is a *voluntary choice*. As proclaimed by the title of one article – "Physicians, Not Conscripts – Conscientious Objection in Health Care"[77] – military conscripts have not chosen to become soldiers; and if they are assigned combat roles, they have not voluntarily accepted those roles or the corresponding role obligations and responsibilities. Exempting conscientious objectors from combat prevents them from being compelled to act against their moral convictions. By contrast, it is argued, when individuals enter the medical profession, they do so voluntarily, and in doing so, they explicitly or implicitly agree to accept the obligations of the profession. Individuals who are conscientiously opposed to providing a legal and professionally accepted medical service have no legitimate claim for accommodation because they can avoid acting against their moral convictions by choosing medical specialties, practice settings, or professions that do not require them to do so.

At most, this line of argument supports the claim that insofar as individuals voluntarily decide to enter the medical profession, they are bound by the corresponding professional obligations. To support an argument against conscientious objection, it must be shown that conscientious refusals are contrary to physicians' professional obligations – a view that will be referred to as *incompatibilism*.

3.2.1 Incompatibilism

Three frequently offered arguments for incompatibilism are based on claims about conscientious refusals and (1) the scope of professional practice; (2) the Patients' Interests First Principle (PIFP); and (3) physicians' obligations to the public.

3.2.1.1 Scope of Professional Practice

Udo Schuklenk and Ricardo Smalling maintain that doctors are obligated to provide all services within the scope of professional practice: "It is implausible that professionals who voluntarily join a profession should be endowed with a legal claim not to provide services that are within the scope of the profession's practice and that society expects them to provide."[78] The alleged implausibility assumes that individuals who voluntarily become physicians accept an obligation to provide all services that are within the scope of the profession's practice and that society reasonably expects them to provide those services. According to Schuklenk and Smalling, there is no place in the medical profession for physicians who are unwilling to fulfill that obligation: "it is reasonable to suggest that doctors refusing to provide professional services that are within the scope of practice should be replaced by someone who is willing to undertake the work."[79]

Assessing these claims requires a definition of "the scope of professional practice." Schuklenk and Smalling do not provide an explicit definition. Surely, however, it would be implausible to claim that all physicians have a professional obligation to provide all legal and professionally accepted medical services. Medicine includes several recognized specialties and subspecialties, and physicians are not obligated to provide medical services that are outside the scope of their specialty or subspecialty. Internists and gynecologists are not obligated to perform cataract surgery. Gastroenterologists and dermatologists are not obligated to offer treatment for pneumonia or schizophrenia. Pediatric oncologists are not obligated to treat adult patients; geriatricians are not obligated to treat infants; and neonatologists are not obligated to provide intensive care for elderly patients.

Indeed, Schuklenk and Smalling appeal to specialization when they claim that physicians can avoid conflicts between their conscience and their professional obligations by choosing a suitable specialty: "Those who object to particular procedures could choose specialties that would not require that they violate their conscience, for example, they could opt for dermatology instead of gynaecology if they are opposed to abortion."[80] By similar reasoning, it might be argued that physicians can limit the scope of their practice even further within chosen specialties and subspecialties. Orthopedic surgeons can limit their practice to hip and knee replacement surgery, shoulder surgery, or foot surgery. Dermatologists can limit their practice to cosmetic or therapeutic reconstructive surgery. Internists and neurologists can limit their practice to the diagnosis and treatment of specified diseases. Gastroenterologists can decide not to offer bariatric surgery. As Holly Fernandez Lynch observes, "not every physician must provide every service within his or her specialty in order to meet professional obligations."[81] Thus, one can ask: If OB–GYNs can decide not to deliver babies without violating their professional obligations, why cannot they also decide not to perform pregnancy terminations if they are morally opposed to abortion? More generally, why do physicians not have the discretion to let their moral convictions guide their decisions about which services to include in the scope of their professional practice?

One answer is to claim that physicians' discretion to limit the services they offer is restricted. This is how Schuklenk and Smalling, among others, respond.[82] They maintain that "it is ultimately up to society to determine the scope of professional practice."[83] To be sure, the discretion of individual physicians is not unlimited. Professional societies, institutions, government agencies, and medical licensing boards are among the social forces that can play a role in determining the scope of professional practice. Nevertheless, the claim that society determines the scope of professional practice appears to undermine rather than support the case against conscientious objection. For, insofar as many, if not all, societies accept (limited) conscientious objection in medicine, it cannot be claimed that conscience-based refusals are *ipso facto* contrary to an obligation to provide all medical services within the scope of (socially determined) professional practice. Michael Robinson advances a similar claim in relation to professional codes of ethics. He claims that insofar as they support accommodation, "it is simply no good arguing that conscientious refusal should not be permitted because physicians voluntarily signed up for these positions [in health professions] and they knew what they were getting into. Indeed, they did! They were getting into a field that explicitly allowed for conscientious refusal."[84]

3.2.1.2 Patients' Interests First Principle (PIFP)

A second argument for incompatibilism is based on a generally recognized principle that physicians have an obligation to put patients' interests or well-being above their own self-interest. This will be referred to as the Patients' Interests First Principle (PIFP). It applies primarily to physicians' obligation to their current (established) patients. The PIFP is endorsed by many professional organizations, including the American Medical Association (AMA) and the UK General Medical Council (GMC). The AMA Code of Medical Ethics states: "physicians' ethical responsibility [is] to place patients' welfare above the physician's own self-interest" (Section 1.1.1).[85] The GMC asserts that good medical practice requires medical professionals to "make the care of patients [their] first concern."[86]

The PIFP can be understood as an implication of the fiduciary model of the physician–patient relationship. Carolyn McLeod draws on that model to defend a prioritizing principle that, like the PIFP, requires the prioritization of patients' interests over the interests of conscientious objectors.[87] She offers two reasons for classifying physicians as fiduciaries – their discretionary authority as gate-keepers of medical services and the vulnerability of patients. She claims that the fiduciary relationship "engenders a duty of loyalty in physicians, that is, a duty to put their patients' health interests first, ahead of their own interests."[88] Other justifications of the PIFP – accounts of why it is a reasonable requirement to impose on anyone who wants to enter the medical profession – include internal morality of medicine,[89] social contract,[90] trust-based,[91] and reciprocal justice[92] accounts. Conceptions of the internal morality of medicine are identified in Section 3.3.1.

In view of the wide recognition of the PIFP, it is not implausible to claim that individuals explicitly or implicitly agree to accept it when they voluntarily enter the medical profession.[93] However, the PIFP is general and needs to be speci-fied. It clearly prohibits physicians from considering their financial interests when making medical recommendations to patients. But beyond that, what are its scope and implications? Specifically, does it support incompatibilism?

Ronit Stahl and Ezekiel Emanuel are among critics of conscientious objec-tion who maintain that conscientious refusal is incompatible with the PIFP.[94] They cite two sections of the AMA Code of Medical Ethics. One (Section 1.1.1, which I have already cited) endorses the PIFP, and the other offers conditional support for conscientious objection. The latter states that, with three specified limitations, "physicians may be able to act (or refrain from acting) in accord-ance with the dictates of their conscience *without violating their professional obligations*" (AMA CEJA 2017, Section 1.1.7; emphasis added). The three limitations are: "Physicians are expected to provide care in emergencies, honor patients' informed decisions to refuse life-sustaining treatment, and respect basic civil liberties and not discriminate against individuals in deciding whether to enter into a professional relationship with a new patient" (AMA CEJA 2017, Section 1.1.7). The Code includes the following additional guideline:

> Several factors impinge on the decision to act according to conscience. Physicians have stronger obligations to patients with whom they have a patient–physician relationship, especially one of long standing; when there is imminent risk of foreseeable harm to the patient or delay in access to treatment would significantly adversely affect the patient's physical or emotional well-being; and when the patient is not reasonably able to access needed treatment from another qualified physician. (AMA CEJA 2017, Section 1.1.7)

Stahl and Emanuel claim that insofar as the Code endorses the PIFP and offers conditional support for conscientious objection, it is "internally inconsistent."[95] However, they do not explain why it is "internally inconsistent" to allow conscientious objection when the guideline and three specified conditions in the AMA Code are satisfied.

Could an incompatibilist plausibly claim that physicians violate the PIFP whenever they conscientiously refuse to provide a medical service? Is it plausible to claim that insofar as objectors' refusals are based in part on *their own* interests (e.g., an interest in maintaining their moral integrity), conscientious refusals are *ipso facto* incompatible with the PIFP and physicians' duty of fidelity to patients? Reflection suggests a negative answer. If physicians could never take their own interests into account without violating their obligations to patients, physicians would not be able to take vacations, refuse to make house calls, limit their practice hours, refuse to expose themselves to excessive financial losses or risks of harm, and so forth. Arguably, this would not be a plausible interpretation of the PIFP and its implications.

Some opponents of conscientious objection have defended incompatibilism by minimizing or trivializing the interests of objectors. For example, Schuklenk and Smalling characterize conscience claims as "essentially arbitrary dislikes,"[96] and Rosamond Rhodes claims that "the doctor who chooses to avoid personal psychic distress declares his willingness to impose burdens of time, inconvenience, financial costs, and rebuke on his patients so that he might feel pure."[97] She claims that objectors' refusals are "for their own comfort," and objectors are "fittingly described as selfish egoists."[98] If the competing interests are characterized in this way – physicians' morally insignificant interests favoring accommodation and patients' morally weighty interests favoring denying accommodation – it would not be implausible to claim that, generally, physicians who refuse to provide medical services that are contrary to their moral convictions violate the PIFP. However, insofar as supporters of accommodation maintain that conscientious refusals are based on (core) moral convictions, they can challenge this characterization of objectors' interests.

An alternative defense of incompatibilism does not trivialize the interests of objectors. Instead, it is claimed that conscientious refusals are incompatible with the PIFP and the fiduciary duty of loyalty to patients because of the harms and burdens that refusals can cause them.

Many incompatibilists claim that conscientious refusals can burden or harm patients by significantly impeding their access to the services that objectors refuse to provide. Patients might be unable to receive (timely) access to those services; locating willing providers can be difficult and time-consuming; patients may have no means of transportation to access willing providers or getting to them can be extremely burdensome. An additional access-related objection focuses on physicians who conscientiously refuse to inform patients about clinically appropriate medical options. If patients are unaware of clinically appropriate medical services, they will not be able to request them; and if physicians conscientiously refuse to offer that information, patients may not receive clinically appropriate medical services. Consequently, it is claimed, conscientious refusals to inform patients can impede access and impose excessive burdens and harms.

Smalling and Schüklenk maintain that "[a]llowing conscientious objection accommodation would invariably lead to reduced access to care and services for patients."[99] They assert that "the most minimally impairing method of achieving timely patient access to care and a functioning healthcare system is to prevent physicians from conscientiously objecting to the provision of legal medical services requested by patients."[100] Their claim may be literally true, but that approach does not consider the importance of conscientious objection and the values at stake. An alternative is to implement measures to ensure that conscientious refusals do not unreasonably impede patient access. Suggested measures will be considered in Section 3.3 on Compatibilism.

Many defenders of accommodation claim that if patients can receive the medical services they want from other providers, conscientious refusals do not harm them. For example, Fernandez Lynch claims that "if patients can be assured of the reasonable availability of services they desire from some competent physician, they are not significantly harmed."[101] In response, Carolyn McLeod argues that even if patients have easy access to medical services from nonobjecting physicians, conscientious refusals can substantially harm them. Like several other important and novel arguments in her 2020 book

Conscience in Reproductive Health Care,[102] her argument about harm merits in-depth critical analysis.

McLeod identifies two types of harm: (1) the "subjective impact" of refusals on patients and (2) loss of trust. As the title of her book indicates, her focus is on reproductive health care. Her argument in relation to the subjective impact of conscientious refusals considers EC and pharmacists, but she maintains that a similar argument applies to physicians who refuse to perform abortions. In both cases, she claims, conscientious refusals can cause similar harms to patients even if they have easy access to the requested service (EC or abortion). Presumably, her argument about harms is also meant to apply to physicians who conscientiously refuse to offer, provide, or prescribe EC.

3.2.1.2.1 Subjective Impact

According to McLeod, determining whether patients are harmed by conscientious refusals to provide EC requires consideration of their social identities and social experiences and "the subjective impact these refusals can have on patients because of how they may be oppressed in society."[103] She identifies two types of subjective impact. One is an increased feeling of social stigma associated with requests for EC. McLeod claims that there is a significant stigma associated with EC due in part to oppressive social stereotypes about women's sexuality. She cites two: "Women who are sexually promiscuous are of low character" and "Women, more so than men, who have unprotected sex are 'irresponsible' or 'careless'."[104] Refusals to provide EC are said to heighten the stigma that patients experience when they request it and cause them to "worry more than they otherwise would about being thought of as bad for wanting EC."[105] Notably, McLeod maintains that this claim about patients' subjective experience does not assume that providers accept such oppressive stereotypes. The second alleged subjective impact is a sense of not being valued by society. McLeod maintains that laws and policies that allow health professionals to conscientiously object to EC can generate a perception among patients that society does not respect them and does not value their ability to control their bodies and their lives. "The subjective impact of conscientious refusals on patients who feel such disrespect," McLeod maintains, "will be severe."[106]

McLeod's argument draws on her claims about the subjective impact on patients as well as Joel Feinberg's (nonnormative) conception of harm as "a setback to interests."[107] As explained in the following paragraphs, she argues that refusing requests for EC can set back women's interests in their reproductive autonomy, moral identity, and sense of security.

Reproductive autonomy. By hypothesis conscientious refusals to provide EC when patients have easy access from other providers do not significantly impede access. Thus, restricted access cannot be the alleged cause of harm. Rather, McLeod claims that patients' interest in reproductive autonomy can be set back when conscientious refusals increase the stigma related to EC – and patients' sense of shame or embarrassment for requesting it is so intense – that they decide against doing so.

Moral identity. A setback to patients' interest in their moral identity is said to occur when refusals feed into oppressive norms that patients have internalized and "vilify them or their behavior."[108] When patients are unable to effectively counter this experienced assault on their moral character, their sense of themselves as morally responsible persons can be threatened.

Sense of security. McLeod claims that when conscientious refusals to provide EC are protected by laws and policies, patients can perceive those refusals as a confirmation that "their society does not respect their ability to govern their body."[109] This is said to be a setback in patients' interest in a sense of security.

What is the evidence for McLeod's claim that conscientious objections can cause the three types of harms she identifies? She admits that "good empirical evidence is lacking about the impact of such conduct [conscientious refusals] on patients," and acknowledges a need "to speculate about its impact, which I do based on various factors, including the power dynamic between health care professionals and patients, and the well-documented stigma that patients experience when they request services like abortions."[110] However, even if it is assumed that she offers plausible scenarios to explain how conscientious refusals *can* harm patients when they have easy access from nonobjecting providers, assessing the ethical implications and practical import of her claims about harm requires answers to three questions: (1) What is the severity of the harm?; (2) Is the harm so severe that causing it is incompatible with justifiable conceptions of the PIFP and physicians' fiduciary obligations?; (3) Is the frequency of the occurrence of situations that are like the scenarios sufficient to justify a presumption against accommodation?

A factor that can affect whether refusals produce the subjective impact McLeod identifies is the way physicians communicate their refusals. If words can matter, there might be ways to communicate refusals that will minimize the risk that they will evoke the kinds of oppressive social stereotypes McLeod cites. Margaret Little and Anne Drapkin Lyerly maintain that the clinician "can indicate what her conviction disallows her from doing without questioning the integrity or moral stature of the patient."[111] They offer the following guidance: "Communication of conscientious objection should be, first and foremost, a statement about the physician, not the patient or her circumstances.

Discussions should be compassionate, respectful, and resolutely first-personal."[112] McLeod is skeptical: Objectors "could try to control the meanings their objections have by explaining what grounds them, but it is clear neither that they should be having discussions of this sort with patients, nor that they would succeed regardless in eliminating an oppressive message from their speech."[113]

Even if, as McLeod claims, offering "unsolicited details about their personal moral beliefs" is unprofessional and unlikely to succeed in eliminating oppressive messages, there are more "neutral" alternatives that she does not consider. For example, clinicians can respond to patients' requests for a medical service by stating that they are unable to provide it. If pressed by patients for an explanation, clinicians can state that their inability to provide the requested service is due to their personal moral beliefs. They might add that there likely are other physicians whose personal moral beliefs allow them to offer the requested service. In any event, McLeod's skepticism about the ability to communicate refusals to patients without unintentionally activating oppressive stereotypes appears to be speculative and is subject to challenge for not giving due consideration to alternative communication strategies, such as the "person-centered" approach recommended by Stephen Buetow and Natalie Gauld.[114] Notably, in her discussion of trust (to be considered in Section 3.2.2.2), McLeod admits that patients may not lose trust in physicians' goodwill when they refuse to perform abortions if they state their refusal in a "respectful and compassionate way."[115]

McLeod's account can be challenged on two additional grounds. First, it can be questioned whether she overestimates the pervasiveness and sway of the oppressive social stereotypes at issue and underestimates the emotional strength and resilience of patients. Second, it can be objected that the scope of patient interests that are said to be relevant is too broad.[116] It is notable that, when McLeod explains her "prioritization approach" to conscientious objection, she identifies patients' *health-care interests* as a subclass of patients' interests that objectors have a fiduciary duty to prioritize over their own interests: "I contend that conscientious objectors in health care have a moral obligation to prioritize the *health care interests* of their patients and the public over their own conscience, and that regulations on conscientious refusals should reflect this fact" (emphasis added).[117] She maintains that the three interests that conscientious refusals allegedly can set back are health-care interests "in the sense that their protection within health care is crucial to patients receiving good, respectful health care."[118] However, if patients have easy access to EC or abortion, and objectors respectfully communicate their objections to patients, what is the basis for claiming that patients will not receive good, respectful care? If the answer cites oppressive social stereotypes that objectors reject, and patients' subjective interpretations of the meaning of refusals are based on those stereotypes, it is doubtful that objectors can be held accountable for patients not receiving "good, respectful health care."

3.2.1.2.2 Loss of Trust

With respect to the alleged harm associated with loss of trust, McLeod claims that trust in their physicians as well as the medical profession is important to patients: "patients have strong interests in being able to trust health care professionals and professions, generally speaking."[119] It would follow, then, that if conscientious refusals undermine patient trust in their physicians and/or the profession, an important interest would be set back, and patients would be harmed.

Drawing on her previous work on trust,[120] and Annette Baier's analysis,[121] McLeod identifies three features of trust: (1) reliance on the competence of the trustee (i.e., the one trusted), (2) reliance on the goodwill of the trustee, and (3) an expectation about shared values. McLeod claims that physicians' conscientious refusals can undermine each of these three features "entirely or to some degree, and therefore can destroy or diminish their [patients'] trust."[122] She also claims that when patients' trust in their physicians is undermined, a consequence can be loss of trust or diminished trust in the profession or other professionals. Notably, none of the features she identifies is a necessary condition – "they may only be common to many instances of trust rather than being necessary for trust."[123]

McLeod supports the claim about conscientious refusals and loss of patient trust by presenting several scenarios in which refusals can jeopardize each of the three features. She presents three scenarios to illustrate how conscientious refusals can undermine the first feature – patients' reliance on their physicians' competence. In one, the cause is unprofessional conduct – a false statement by the objecting physician that abortions threaten patients' health by causing breast cancer or depression. To be sure, a patient who knows or later learns that this is misinformation *should* lose trust in the physician's competence. But this loss of trust is due to the physician's false statement, not to the refusal to perform the requested abortion. A similar observation applies to a second scenario. In that scenario, the physician who refuses to provide a requested abortion treats the patient "shabbily – without an ounce of sympathy."[124] The physician's lack of "moral competence" is said to demonstrate a lack of trustworthiness. However, it is the physician's attitude and behavior, not the refusal to provide a requested abortion that undermines trust.

In a third scenario, OB–GYNs who conscientiously object to abortion opted out of abortion training when they were residents and now lack the competencies needed to terminate pregnancies. Undoubtedly, their patients cannot rely on their competence to perform abortions, but patients might still reasonably rely on their competence to provide other OB–GYN services, such as prenatal care and gynecological examinations. McLeod speculates that "patients are likely to be cautious about relying on physicians' competence in general after witnessing their incompetence in a specific area."[125] This is an empirical claim for which no evidence is offered. However, it might be more important to ask whether diminished trust in other areas is *reasonable* or *warranted*. Unless it is, the extent to which objectors may be held responsible for undermining patient trust and any resulting harm is questionable.

McLeod acknowledges that objectors can avoid doing or saying anything that jeopardizes patients' reliance on their clinical or moral competence:

> [C]onscientious refusals need not reveal to patients that objectors lack competence, of a non-moral or moral variety. The objectors may not claim to be technically incompetent or say anything that indicates a lack of such competence, or even do anything that signals a deficiency in moral competence. The objectors may show enough sympathy for their patients that the patients do not lose confidence in their ability to be morally responsible.[126]

Thus, what objectors say or do not say or do or do not do – not the refusal per se – can be decisive in determining whether conscientious refusals undermine patients' reliance on physicians' competence.

McLeod understands goodwill as "care or concern for the other . . . In trusting people, we rely on their good will, so understood."[127] Focusing on abortion, McLeod explains how conscientious refusals to provide abortions *can* prompt patients to question whether to continue to rely on their physicians' goodwill toward them. However, she once again admits that what objectors do or do not do or say or do not say can be decisive in determining whether conscientious refusals undermine patients' reliance on physicians' goodwill:

> [P]atients can assume that physicians who conscientiously refuse their requests for abortion services still feel goodwill toward them. The physicians might give them a proper referral for an abortion, for example, which in turn allows them to continue to rely on their physician's goodwill. The physicians might also state their refusal in such a respectful and compassionate way – a way that deflects any stigma the patients might experience – that the patients are not left questioning their goodwill.[128]

The last of the three features of trust is shared values: "Usually, in trusting people, we expect them to share enough of (or enough of a commitment to) our values that we can indeed trust them."[129] Conscientious refusals, McLeod claims, "can damage patients' trust . . . by undermining their expectation

about shared values."[130] To be sure, patients who request pregnancy terminations and physicians who refuse to provide them for reasons of conscience do
not share the same ethical beliefs about abortion. However, patients who request
abortions and physicians who refuse to provide them can continue to have
shared values about health and health care that are unrelated to abortion. For
example, a patient who has had a five-year trusting relationship with her OB–
GYN might decide to continue trusting them to provide routine gynecological
care despite their conscientious refusal to provide a requested abortion. Whether
the scope of shared values is wide enough to maintain patient trust is largely
a subjective patient judgment.

There are several areas in health care other than abortion that are potential
sources of mismatch between physicians' and patients' values, including political values, beliefs about vaccination, approaches to end of life care, and beliefs
about alternative medicine. When there are mismatches, generally it is not
physicians' responsibility or fiduciary duty to align their values with patients'
values to maintain patient trust and prevent harms that can result from loss of
trust. McLeod does not disagree. She only requires objectors "to ensure that
patients who request standard services that are medically indicated for them
receive these services, either from the [objecting] professionals themselves or
from a trustworthy colleague."[131] Arguably, preventing loss of patient trust is
not the exclusive responsibility of physicians. Depending on the circumstances,
patients may be able to avoid entering into relationships with physicians whose
values are incompatible with earning and maintaining their trust.

McLeod concedes that conscientious refusals can *enhance* rather than damage trust:

> [H]ealth care professionals who make a conscientious objection without
> revealing a lack of competence and goodwill could be trusted more by their
> patients as a result, not to provide the service that morally offends them to be
> sure, but to provide other health care services. The reason for this heightened
> trust would be the openness and honesty that the objectors display about their
> values.[132]

This statement affirms that it can be what physicians do or do not do or say or do
not say when they refuse to provide medical services – and not their conscientious refusals per se – that harms patients by undermining trust.

3.2.1.3 Obligations to the Public

The PIFP applies primarily to physicians' obligations to current (established)
patients. McLeod extends the incompatibilist critique to include physicians'
obligations to members of the public who are not their current patients. She

defines the public as "the group or collective made up of individuals who live in the jurisdiction where the health care professionals in question are licensed to practice."[133] She maintains that physicians' fiduciary duty to the public precludes them "from allowing their conscience to dictate who becomes their patient in circumstances where they cannot ensure (e.g., by giving proper referrals) that prospective patients will receive the health care they need."[134] She does not endorse strict incompatibility between conscientious refusals and physicians' obligations to the public. However, in view of the substantial restrictions she proposes, her position can be classified as qualified incompatibilism.

McLeod's account of professional obligations to the public is based on licensing board mandates and the conception of physicians as fiduciaries. She maintains that licensing boards typically charge physicians with promoting public health and (equitable) access to health care. Promoting these ends is a condition of licensure, and their promotion is a responsibility of the medical profession and its members. Professional organizations generally recognize this obligation. However, even if it is acknowledged that physicians have an unspecified obligation to promote public health and (equitable) access to health care, the implications for conscientious objection are unclear.

To further specify physicians' obligations to the public, McLeod applies the fiduciary model. Her justification for considering physicians to be fiduciaries for the public is twofold. First, licensing boards give physicians discretionary authority in their gatekeeping role over how to discharge their obligations to the public. Second, members of the public are vulnerable, and physicians have the power to take advantage of that vulnerability by exploiting or abusing their discretionary authority: "Whenever one has discretionary power over another's interests, there is a chance that one will exploit them, or, in other words, take unfair advantage of their vulnerable state. The need to guard against this risk is what morally grounds the fiduciary duty of loyalty."[135]

As McLeod understands the fiduciary duty of loyalty in this context, it is owed to the public collectively, not to any individual member; and physicians are obligated to give priority to the goals of public health and (equitable) access over their own interests. What are the implications for conscientious objection? McLeod offers a three-condition answer: (1) physicians who conscientiously refuse to provide a medical service requested by a person who is not a current patient have an obligation to ensure that the person "understand[s] where else they can obtain it nearby";[136] (2) if there are no available providers of the refused service in the area, "the professionals themselves should complain to their profession" which "must share with them the burden of promoting equit-able access;"[137] (3) When no other physicians are available, physicians "should, out of fidelity to their mandate, do it anyway."[138]

McLeod's specification of conscientious objectors' fiduciary duties to the public can be challenged. By hypothesis, physicians have discretion as gatekeepers. It is that discretion and the vulnerability of members of the public to exploitation and abuse that is said to justify conceptualizing physicians as fiduciaries of the public – specifically in relation to their interest in public health and (equitable) access to health care. It can be argued that the duties to promote public health and access are discretionary (imperfect) duties in the sense that physicians can decide when, how, and in what contexts to fulfill them. In instances where OB–GYNs have no moral objection to abortion, they might decide to fulfill their obligation to promote public health and access to health care by offering pregnancy terminations. By contrast, OB–GYNs who are morally opposed to abortion might decide to fulfill their obligations to promote public health and access by providing women's health services that do not include abortion. Those in both categories might plausibly claim that they are acting as fiduciaries for the public insofar as they give priority to the public's interests within the scope of health-care services that they offer. Both can plausibly claim that they are fulfilling their fiduciary duty to refrain from abusing or exploiting members of the public. Arguably, an unspecified duty to promote public health and access to health care cannot ground a duty to provide specified services, such as abortion or MAID.

An additional problem is associated with the third condition, which states that the profession must share "the burden of promoting equitable access." McLeod does not explain what that means in practice. Fernandez Lynch proposes an institutional approach to conscientious objection that addresses this issue. Her approach is discussed in Section 3.3.2.

3.2.2 Additional Objections

Three additional objections cite: (1) the alleged impact of conscientious refusals on third parties; (2) a concern about licensing discrimination; and (3) slippery slope worries.

3.2.2.1 Impact on Third Parties

Opposition to conscientious objection is not limited to concerns about the impact on patients and prospective patients. In addition, concerns have been expressed about the impact on third parties, such as nonobjecting physicians, administrators, and health-care institutions. In relation to them, obviously, the concern is not about access. Rather, it is that conscientious refusals might impose unreasonable burdens on them.

Within health-care institutions, to prevent conscientious refusals from impeding patient access to the range of medical services that an institution is committed to offering, nonobjectors must provide the services that objectors refuse to provide.[139] Thus, it is claimed, accommodating objectors without impeding patient access can impose unfair burdens on nonobjectors.[140] Even if physicians who provide the medical services do not object morally, it can be claimed that satisfying the demand can be burdensome for them. For example, if an intensive care unit (ICU) physician who objects to participating in donation after circulatory determination of death (DCDD) or palliative sedation to unconsciousness is accommodated, other intensivists may be required to be on call more often and work additional and/or more inconvenient hours. In some cases, accommodating objectors without negatively affecting patient care might require hiring additional staff, which can strain an institution's budget. In some situations, making staff changes to accommodate objectors can place an unreasonable burden on department heads.

To be sure, fairness and not imposing unreasonable burdens on third parties are legitimate concerns. No health professional or no entity should be required to shoulder unreasonable burdens to enable objectors to maintain their moral integrity. However, addressing concerns about fairness and unreasonable burdens within health-care institutions does not require a blanket policy against accommodation. Such concerns can be addressed instead by implementing constraints on accommodation. Policies can stipulate that requests for accommodation will be approved only if it will not impose an excessive burden on other physicians. Similar constraints can protect department heads and institutions from excessive burdens.[141]

Concerns about unreasonable burdens and fairness extend beyond the impact on colleagues who practice within the same health-care institution. For example, Schuklenk and Smalling maintain that Canadian physicians who are willing to provide services that objectors refuse to provide "carry an inequitable load of such work."[142] To evaluate claims about inequity, it is important to keep in mind that objectors are only refusing to provide some medical services – those that are contrary to their moral convictions. They are providing other medical services. For example, physicians who conscientiously refuse to offer MAID might offer palliative care, and OB–GYNs who conscientiously refuse to terminate pregnancies might offer routine gynecological care or specialize in gynecological oncology. Objectors may not be sharing the burdens of providing services they refuse to provide, but they are sharing the burden of providing other medical services and promoting the public's health. In this respect, the difference between objectors and nonobjectors can be understood as a difference in specializations.

Some specializations require longer hours, are more stressful, and more emotionally and physically demanding. Physicians may choose such specialties for a variety of reasons. They might consider them to be more interesting, more important from a public health perspective, more challenging, and/or more rewarding. In any event, when physicians do not choose such specialties, it does not follow that they are responsible for imposing unreasonable burdens on those who do. Similarly, if objectors are providing medical services that contribute to a population's health, it does not follow that when they refuse to offer medical services that are contrary to their moral convictions they are responsible for imposing unreasonable burdens on physicians who voluntarily offer those services.

Granted, some physicians may feel obligated to see more patients and work longer hours to satisfy the need for services that objectors do not provide. However, this is not significantly different from primary care physicians or general practitioners who feel obligated to see more patients and extend practice hours because their supply in an area is insufficient to meet patient demand due to factors other than conscientious objection. To deny accommodation to objectors so that nonobjectors will not feel the need to voluntarily increase their workload would be like not allowing orthopedic surgeons to refuse to offer elbow and knee surgery because orthopedists who do offer those services might feel a need to voluntarily increase their workloads to meet patient demand. Generally, in the absence of regulations that require physicians to take on extra patients and work extra hours to meet the demand for a medical service, accommodating conscientious objection does not give rise to substantially more inequities in workloads than physicians' choices of specialties, subspecialties, and practice locations. A proposal that aims to promote an alignment between patient demand and physician supply that does not require a choice between imposing unreasonable burdens on nonobjectors or denying accommodation to conscientious objectors is examined in Section 3.3.2.

Some commentators have proposed an alternative service requirement modeled on a similar requirement for conscientious objectors to military service. For example, Christopher Meyers and Robert Woods call for an "alternative form of public-benefiting professional service;"[143] and, with some modifications, Robert Card endorses their proposal.[144] Meyers and Woods state that the goal "is to require some service that is both of comparable social benefit and, to most physicians, similarly 'distasteful'."[145] This proposal is subject to two challenges. First, the "similarly distasteful" requirement can be questioned. Although many draftees may find military service "distasteful" – especially if it involves combat – it is unlikely that nonobjectors who voluntarily choose to provide medical services that objectors refuse to provide find those services "distasteful." Is the intent perhaps to punish objectors for refusing to provide specific medical services? If so, the justification is questionable. Arguably, if objectors act wrongly, denying accommodation is a more appropriate response. Second, there is an important difference between conscientious objectors to military service and conscientious objectors in medicine. Absent an alternative service requirement, there is no assurance that the former provide significant public service. However, physicians who conscientiously refuse to provide some medical services do provide others and, like nonobjectors, promote the public's health.[146]

3.2.2.2 Discrimination

Some opponents of conscientious objection claim that accommodating conscientious objectors will license discrimination. As an opponent of conscientious objection expresses this concern, "The door to 'value-driven medicine' is a door to a Pandora's box of idiosyncratic, bigoted, discriminatory medicine."[147]

It is incontestable that discrimination is unacceptable in health care. It is one thing for physicians to refuse to provide specific medical services (e.g., abortion, EC, or palliative sedation to unconsciousness) and quite another to refuse to provide medical services to Black or Muslim patients and yet be willing to provide the same medical services to white or Christian patients. It is a settled view – based on defensible and widely shared conceptions of justice, equality, dignity, and respect – that racial, ethnic, religious, and gender-based prejudices or biases are ethically wrong. Even if they are conscience-based (i.e., rooted in fundamental moral beliefs), accommodation for objections based on such discriminatory beliefs is unjustified.

However, a blanket policy of nonaccommodation risks throwing out the baby with the bathwater. Policies that allow conscientious objection can clearly state that they do not license discrimination. For example, the section of the AMA Code of Ethics that addresses conscientious objection includes the following statement: "In following conscience, physicians should: . . . Take care that their actions do not discriminate against or unduly burden individual patients" (AMA CEJA 2017, Section 1.1.7). Statements such as this illustrate how conscientious objection policies that offer qualified accommodation can avoid licensing invidious discrimination.

It is, of course, possible to question whether a particular specification of the scope of prohibited discrimination is justified. For example, it was not until 1993 that the AMA included sexual orientation in the scope of prohibited discrimination;[148] and it was not until 2007 that gender identify was included.[149] This expansion indicates that the scope of prohibited discrimination within a profession can change over time. Such changes correspond to changes in accepted views within and outside the profession about the scope of prohibited discrimination and justified limits on conscientious objection.

3.2.2.3 Slippery Slope

Schuklenk and Smalling present a version of a slippery slope argument against accommodation in liberal democracies.[150] Such societies, they claim, "rightly do not take a stance on the substance of their citizens' moral or religious or other convictions."[151] This constraint on evaluating objectors' reasons, "opens the door to any number of more or less arbitrary and random conscientious objection claims"[152] and provides no opportunity to distinguish between conscience-based objections that do and do not provide a *pro tanto* moral reason for accommodation. A blanket policy of nonaccommodation will forestall having to accommodate "any number of idiosyncratic private views of the universe and on what may or may not be ethically acceptable."[153]

To some extent, this objection misses the point of accommodating conscientious objectors, which is to provide physicians with diverse/idiosyncratic ethical beliefs moral space in which to practice medicine in accordance with those beliefs. Moreover, the authors fail to provide evidence that a substantial number of doctors are likely to make "arbitrary and random conscientious objection claims." Evidence is needed to support such a skeptical and unflattering view of members of the medical profession. The authors also fail to consider that constraints on accommodation designed to protect patients and other physicians and prevent discrimination can provide friction to substantially reduce the slope's slipperiness.

Even if the authors are correct to claim that it is unwarranted to evaluate "the truth or even plausibility of objectors' ethical beliefs,"[154] it does not follow that no assessment of their beliefs is warranted. Arguments in support of requiring objectors to provide a justification are considered in Section 4.

3.3 Compatibilism

There are two types of compatibilism. One, based on a conception of the end of medicine, rejects the incompatibilist view that conscientious refusals are contrary to the professional obligations of physicians if they prevent patients from having timely access to medical services that are legal and compatible with current professional standards. The other type of compatibilism accepts that view and maintains that measures can be put into place to protect patient access and prevent conflicts between conscientious refusals and professional obligations. There are two approaches to this second type of compatibilism. One proposes constraints on accommodation to protect access. The second (an institutional approach) assigns to medical licensing boards the primary responsibility for preventing conscientious objection from impeding a population's access.

3.3.1 The End of Medicine

Farr Curlin and Christopher Tollefsen maintain that refusal to provide medical services that commonly trigger conscientious objections, such as abortion, contraception, and MAID, is justified because those practices are not consistent with the "Way of Medicine" – their conception of the internal morality of medicine.[155] According to the Way of Medicine, health is the exclusive end or goal of medicine. The authors argue that services such as abortion, contraception, and MAID do not promote health. Consequently, individual physicians do not have an obligation to provide such services, and it cannot be claimed that refusing to provide them is incompatible with their professional obligations. Moreover, insofar as medical services do not promote health, it cannot be maintained that individual physicians or the medical profession have an obligation to protect patient access to them.

The notion of an internal morality of medicine has generated substantial disagreement. To cite a few examples. Edmund Pellegrino endorses an essentialist view, according to which there is a timeless morality of medicine based on the nature of medicine as a healing profession and the vulnerability of patients.[156] Fred Miller and Howard Brody advocate an evolutionary conception, according to which the internal morality of medicine is subject to reinterpretation in response to changing circumstances.[157] John Arras questions the usefulness of the concept;[158] and Robert Veatch argues that since the ends of medicine are in part socially constructed, there is no *internal* morality of medicine.[159] Social contract, trust-based, reciprocity, and negotiation are among the theories that offer accounts of professional obligations that are not based on an alleged internal morality of medicine.[160]

Curlin and Tollefsen defend their Way of Medicine conception by contrasting it with a consumerist conception of medicine – the "provider of services model" (PSM). It provides the following account of professional obligations: "if an intervention is permitted by law, is technologically possible, and is autonomously desired by the patient, medical physicians should provide the intervention. Indeed, they may be professionally obligated to do so."[161] The authors argue that insofar as this conception of professional obligations fails to recognize health as the exclusive end of medicine, it fails to promote patient–physician trust, protect patient health, or prevent abuses.

The authors' defense of the Way of Medicine model and compatibilism can be challenged for presenting a false choice between two extremes: an expansive and rudderless conception of medicine and a narrow and controversial conception of an internal morality of medicine. Arguably, one can reject the consumerist PSM without endorsing an extremely narrow and controversial conception of medicine.

The authors' defense of compatibilism can also be challenged for its reliance on a controversial conception of health – a contested concept.[162] Their defense is based on a narrow and controversial conception of health as "an objective bodily norm and as an objective human good."[163] As they explain it, citing Leon Kass, health is to be understood "in a limited, circumscribed, and embodied sense: what Kass describes as 'the well-working of the organism as a whole,' realized and manifested in the characteristic activities of the living body in accordance with its species-specific life-form."[164] The authors' claim that services that commonly trigger conscientious refusals, such as abortion, contraception, and MAID, do not promote health is based on this narrow and controversial conception of health.

There is an additional reason to question Curlin and Tollefsen's defense of compatibilism. The practice of medicine takes place in the context of institutional rules that ground expectations for health-care providers and patients. If physicians rely on Curlin and Tollefsen's conception of the internal morality of medicine to justify refusing to provide a legal and professionally accepted medical service, they substitute their own understanding of the scope of acceptable medical practice for the current institutional understanding of it. To be sure, institutional standards may be mistaken, and they are subject to critical scrutiny and revision. Arguably, however, as members of the medical profession physicians should not expect to be free, unilaterally, to substitute their understanding of the scope of acceptable medical practice for that of the profession. An aim of two other defenses of compatibilism – proposed constraints on accommodation and an institutional approach – is to allow physicians to practice in accordance with their (unorthodox) conception of medicine while assuring that patients receive currently accepted medical services.

3.3.2 Constraints on Accommodation

One proposed set of constraints is referred to as the "conventional compromise." As Dan Brock explains it, conscientious refusals will be accommodated only if three conditions are satisfied: (1) the physician informs the patient about the service if it is clinically relevant (the disclosure requirement); (2) the physician refers the patient to a health professional who is willing and able to provide the service (the referral requirement); (3) the referral does not impose an unreasonable burden on the patient.[165] The third requirement reflects the recognition that even if the disclosure and referral conditions are satisfied, patients can face insurmountable obstacles or substantial burdens to access due to travel time and/or distance, lack of convenient access to transportation, and so forth. Together, the three conditions aim to protect easy access – ensuring that conscientious refusals do not unreasonably impede patient access to clinically indicated medical services.

The "conventional compromise" can be challenged. Incompatibilists can maintain that protecting easy access is not sufficient because patients also have an interest in a continued relationship with their physicians.[166] Notably, however, as proponents of this argument will acknowledge, it is limited to ongoing relationships and does not apply to objectors who refuse to provide services to patients with whom they do not have an established relationship. In addition, it can be questioned whether any plausible specifications of the PIFP and physicians' fiduciary duties imply that patients' interest in maintaining a relationship with their doctors trumps the latters' interest in practicing medicine without violating their moral convictions.

"Preventive ethics"[167] might mitigate the concern about the impact of conscientious refusals on ongoing doctor–patient relationships. Objectors can practice preventive ethics by informing prospective patients prior to establishing a relationship with them that there are specified services that they do not offer. For example, OB–GYNs who have a conscientious objection to abortion can take steps to make sure that prospective patients are aware that they do not terminate pregnancies. This information might be communicated routinely by office staff when prospective patients call for information or a first appointment; it might be prominently displayed in the waiting room on a list of services members of the practice do and do not offer; or it might be communicated in person during the initial visit.

A challenge to the "conventional compromise" from the perspective of objectors claims that it fails to offer accommodation that is acceptable to them.[168] Objectors can claim that disclosure and referral will make them complicit in moral wrongdoing and will undermine their moral integrity. Julian Savulescu and Udo Schuklenk, cite this concern as a reason why objectors would reject the conventional compromise: "If you believe that abortion constitutes the murder of a human person, a 'compromise' that would oblige you to pass the pregnant women on to a colleague who you know would be willing to commit the 'murder', evidently does not constitute a viable compromise."[169] A similar moral complicity objection applies to the disclosure condition. McLeod also rejects a compromise approach, arguing that a genuine compromise requires a resolution that is satisfactory to all parties; and it is infeasible to find a middle ground that is acceptable to objectors.[170]

There are two responses to the moral complicity objection. First, objectors' claims about moral complicity can be questioned.[171] However, as explained in Section 2.1, there are competing conceptions of complicity and, consistent with the aims of accommodation, it is arguable that considerable deference should be given to objectors' conceptions. Second, in response to objectors' complaints that disclosure or referral would undermine their moral integrity, it can be stated that insofar as either is needed to facilitate easy access, failing to provide it is incompatible with any plausible specifications of the PIFP and physicians' fiduciary duties to their patients.

Finally, compatibilists can challenge the conventional compromise by arguing that the need for the disclosure and referral requirements is context dependent.[172] Insofar as the primary goal of both is to ensure that refusals do not result in patients' lack of easy access, it is argued that if patients can have easy access without requiring disclosure or referral there is no compelling reason to require either. This suggests substituting an outcome-focused requirement for the act-focused disclosure and referral requirements: disclosure and referral are required when patients would otherwise not have easy access to the services that objectors refuse to provide. In some cases, neither might be required. For example, disclosure is not needed when patients request or ask about a medical service. However, in many cases it might not be feasible for objectors to ascertain whether easy access requires disclosure or referral. Accordingly, to protect patient access, an alternative to disclosure or referral requirements is a rebuttable presumption in favor of both. Rebutting the presumption would require a reasonable belief that patients do not need disclosure or referral. If patients ask about options or request a referral, it is arguable that plausible specifications of the PIFP and physicians' fiduciary duties to their patients require providing the requested information and assistance – or at least telling patients how to get them.

3.3.3 An Institutional Approach

Holly Fernandez Lynch advocates an "institutional compromise" that aims to protect access without significantly limiting conscientious objection.[173] Since the United States provides the basic institutional context for her analysis, its generalizability can be questioned.

Whereas the "conventional compromise" places the primary responsibility on objectors for ensuring that conscientious refusals do not unreasonably impede patient access, Fernandez Lynch's institutional compromise assigns that responsibility to the *medical profession*. She claims that in virtue of its monopoly on most medical services and the substantial gatekeeping role of its members, the profession has an obligation to protect access to designated medical services (i.e., services to which all members of the public should have access); and it is the responsibility of the medical profession to ensure that conscientious objection does not impede access to designated medical services. Notably, this is a collective obligation of the profession, not an obligation of individual objectors.

Fernandez Lynch maintains that licensing boards are "the most appropriate representative of the medical profession as a collective whole."[174] Accordingly, she ascribes to them the medical profession's responsibility to protect access. A first step is for licensing boards to specify the medical services to which all members of the public should have access (designated medical services). However, their decisions about the scope of these services are subject to legal and scientific constraints. The list of designated medical services cannot include any that are illegal or "scientifically incapable of accomplishing the patient's goal"; and legislatures can specify services "for which boards *must* satisfy patient demand."[175] Licensing board decisions about the scope of designated medical services that are not based solely on considerations of legality and "scientific propriety" must be subject to a fair deliberative process that includes stakeholders outside the medical profession.

Consistent with Fernandez Lynch's view that licensing boards are the most appropriate representative of the medical profession, she also assigns to them the responsibility to implement measures that will enable the profession to satisfy its obligation to prevent conscientious objection from impeding access to designated medical services. To discharge this obligation, licensing boards need to determine whether the supply of physicians in a geographic area is sufficient to meet the demand for designated services in that geographic area. To facilitate determining the effect of conscientious refusals on supply, licensing boards are tasked with identifying objectors and the services they refuse to provide. Fernandez Lynch proposes requiring conscientious objectors to register with licensing boards at the point of licensure and whenever their ethical beliefs change. It is the responsibility of licensing boards to decide whether physicians who register as conscientious objectors qualify for exemptions. Boards may refuse to grant objector status for a limited number of reasons, including lack of sincerity and to prevent invidious discrimination. Fernandez Lynch maintains that determining who qualifies for an exemption is independent of considerations of access. Generally, apart from rejecting discriminatory beliefs, Fernandez Lynch does not endorse assessing the validity of beliefs. Unlike some commentors, whose views are examined in Section 4, she does not recommend requiring objectors to publicly explain and justify their reasons.

Licensing boards are also assigned the responsibility of determining whether people who live in a geographic area have "reasonable access" to designated medical services. Fernandez Lynch acknowledges that access is not exclusively a function of distance to available providers. Other factors she considers include emotional and psychological burdens, such as those that can be associated with changing physicians, and accessibility (e.g., access to transportation). This gives rise to a dilemma that Fernandez Lynch does not address. On the one hand, a fine-grained criterion that is tailored to capture the realities of patients' lives is needed to fully capture the barriers to access as they experience them. On the other hand, the more fine-grained the criteria, the more challenging it will be for licensing boards to determine whether access is sufficient and to correct mismatches between supply and demand. As a practical matter, managing the distribution of physicians in a geographical area to prevent or remedy supply and demand mismatches appears to favor a criterion of reasonable access that is coarse- rather than fine-grained.

Fernandez Lynch claims that once geographic boundaries are established, "it will be possible to determine ... when a patient is forced to go beyond the decided-on geographic boundary to obtain care *as a result of conscientious refusals* by doctors within that boundary" (emphasis added).[176] However, this claim implausibly assumes that the shortfall is due exclusively to conscientious objection. Mismatches between supply and demand can be due (in part) to other factors such as physicians' choice of practice locations and specialties. The following hypothetical case illustrates this point. Abortion is among the designated medical services in geographical area GA_1. There are too few OB–GYNs in GA_1 to provide sufficient access to abortion for women who live in GA_1. There are thirty OB–GYNs in GA_1. Of these, ten do not provide pregnancy terminations; five are registered conscientious refusers; three do not terminate pregnancies because they fear protests and acts of violence from antiabortion activists; and two do not perform abortions due to their subspecialties (oncology and urology). The licensing board calculates that twenty-eight OB–GYNs who are willing to perform abortions would be needed to satisfy demand in GA_1. Thus, some women will be forced to go beyond that geographical boundary to receive an abortion. It is misleading to claim that they are forced to do so by doctors' conscientious refusals. What are the licensing board's obligations in this case? Is it obligated only to attempt to facilitate adding five willing OB–GYNs to make up for the shortfall within GA_1 due to conscientious refusals? Since the impact on women's access is the same regardless of the reason OB–GYNs do not perform pregnancy terminations, why should the obligation of licensing boards to remedy mismatches in supply and demand be limited to those that are attributable exclusively to conscientious refusals?

Fernandez Lynch maintains that if a licensing board ascertains that access is insufficient in a geographical area due to conscientious refusals, they have an obligation "to remedy the mismatch."[177] Among the measures that she claims medical licensing boards can use as remedies, most need to be implemented by, or in conjunction with, other entities such as the federal government, medical schools, and professional organizations. These measures include a variety of financial and other incentives. None are coercive. Some are modeled on government programs to rectify physician shortages in health professional shortage areas (HPSAs). They include awarding scholarships and loan forgiveness to students and professionals who commit to practice in HPSAs and bonuses for providing services to Medicare beneficiaries who live in those areas. Fernandez Lynch suggests that licensing boards "perhaps in conjunction with medial schools and professional organizations, could implement similar programs for students and physicians willing to provide needed and unpopular services in analogous 'moral diversity shortage areas'."[178]

Fernandez Lynch does not endorse adopting a modified version of medical school admissions policies that give preference to applicants who make a commitment to practice in rural and other underserved areas. Her primary reason is a concern that adapting this model to remedy mismatches in "moral diversity shortage areas" would tend to exclude conscientious refusers from the profession "at the front end." She prefers offering incentives "at the back end" (i.e., after earning MD degrees), such as loan forgiveness to those who practice in areas in need of nonobjectors. She also endorses programs in medical schools like those in law schools in relation to legal aid and pro bono work that have the aim of "shaping student preferences in a way that corresponds to social needs."[179] Another proposed measure that requires the involvement of other entities is for licensing boards to "work with the federal government" to implement immigration programs "aimed at attracting willing international physicians."[180]

Suggested direct actions by licensing boards include increasing the use of telemedicine to remedy mismatches by reducing requirements for providing care via telemedicine across state lines; subsidizing the travel costs of patients who need to travel outside their designated geographic area; and allowing members of other health professions (e.g., nurse physicians, midwives, and physician assistants [PAs]) to provide services for which there is a mismatch between supply and demand.

Fernandez Lynch's account of measures to remedy mismatches between supply and demand is problematic for four reasons. First, it is questionable whether licensing boards have the authority, power, or influence needed to affect the policies and practices of entities such as the government, medical schools, and professional organizations. Second, insofar as licensing boards lack the power to implement measures to remedy mismatches as well as the authority to compel other entities to implement them, it is misleading to claim that they – rather than those other entities – bear the primary responsibility for remedying mismatches. Insofar as "ought implies can," licensing boards cannot be said to have an obligation to remedy mismatches. At most, it can be said that licensing boards have an obligation to undertake efforts to influence the policies and practices of relevant entities such as legislatures, government agencies, medical schools, and professional organizations. Third, as Fernandez Lynch acknowledges, there may be lag times between the detection of mismatches and the implementation of effective remedies. As a result, patients will experience impediments to access, even if only temporarily. Depending on the circumstances, lag times can be substantial and, due to changes in supply and demand, recurrent. Fourth, putting aside the problem of lag time, even if the specific measures that Fernandez Lynch suggests could be implemented, it is questionable that they could substantially remedy or prevent mismatches.

Fernandez Lynch acknowledges that her institutional approach will require "a fundamental restructuring of licensing boards and their responsibilities, including the development of new levels of expertise, as well as a significant investment of resources."[181] She also acknowledges that there are substantial political hurdles to achieving the required fundamental restructuring. In response, she states, "we must not be bound by the current political winds. Instead, normative correctness should be our primary guide, and that criterion is satisfied."[182] However, if the aim is to remedy or prevent impediments to access without significantly limiting conscientious objection, it is doubtful whether this is achievable by restructuring that only requires or enables licensing boards to implement the measures she identifies. Achieving that aim in the United States may require more fundamental and comprehensive institutional restructuring.

Although Fernandez Lynch's primary focus is on the obligations of licensing boards as a representative of the medical profession, she considers some questions about the obligations of objectors. Most noteworthy is her discussion of objectors' obligations in what she refers to as "hard cases" – cases in which licensing boards fail to prevent or remedy a mismatch between supply and demand with the result that if objectors do not provide a requested service, patients will not have access to it. She maintains that in a hypothetical "last doctor in town" scenario in which there is only one physician – an objector – who can provide the service at issue, the objector has an obligation to provide it despite their conscientious objection. In this situation, she argues, the objector is the "sole gatekeeper" and "bears the profession's monopoly power and concomitant obligation to preserve patient access."[183] If there is more than one objector who could provide the service, Fernandez Lynch suggests a lottery to determine who should be considered the last doctor in town. Notably, although Fernandez Lynch argues that objectors in hard cases can have an *obligation* to provide services despite their conscientious objections, she offers several reasons against compelling compliance or subjecting objectors who refuse to comply to legal penalties or disciplinary action. Instead, she endorses holding licensing boards liable for failing to discharge their obligation to prevent or remedy mismatches. For the reasons offered, however, if licensing boards are limited to the measures Fernandez Lynch suggests, the extent of their responsibility for mismatches and patients' lack of access is unclear. It is arguable that the entities who fail to implement measures proposed by licensing boards bear some, if not most, of the responsibility.

4 Assessing Objectors' Beliefs and Reasons

Compatibilists generally agree that objectors should not be accommodated if their beliefs are racist or demonstrably false. Many also maintain a similar position with respect to beliefs that are incompatible with the core goals of medicine (e.g., promoting health and alleviating pain). If there is any disagreement about these three constraints, it is primarily about measures to ascertain whether objectors' refusals are based on any of the disqualifying beliefs – for example, whether formal review board oversight should be required. Similarly, compatibilists typically require grounding moral beliefs to satisfy a "genuineness" requirement. Beyond these points of agreement, however, there is substantial disagreement about belief-related requirements. A hotly debated question is whether objectors should be required to provide a justification by explaining their grounding reasons.

4.1 Genuineness

According to a standard conception, conscientious objections are genuine only if they are *moral* objections. This requirement excludes objections based on other considerations, such as financial or aesthetic reasons.[184] Beyond this threshold requirement, genuineness is typically primarily understood to be a function of the sincerity and depth of objectors' grounding moral beliefs.[185]

Lori Kantymir and Carolyn McLeod do not require all objectors to demonstrate that they satisfy a genuineness condition. They maintain that if objectors are required to provide justifications, they should be given the option to demonstrate only that their objection is *reasonable* "by showing that what grounds the objection is as likely or more likely to be true than what grounds the standard of care for patients."[186] Thus, to be granted accommodation for satisfying the reasonableness condition, objectors would need to demonstrate that there is good reason to question existing clinical norms and standards. The authors propose this reasonableness option to provide an opportunity for objectors to challenge accepted clinical standards and norms, to advocate for change, and to promote change by fostering necessary awareness. Insofar as this reasonableness standard is the basis for granting accommodation, the primary aim would not be to give physicians moral space in which to practice medicine in accordance with their distinctive personal moral beliefs.

For Kimberly Brownlee, a key question related to the sincerity and depth of a moral conviction is whether it satisfies what she refers to as "the communicative principle of conscientiousness."[187] Two of the four conditions of the principle are particularly relevant in the current context. One, a "non-evasion condition," requires a willingness to bear the risks of honoring one's moral conviction. This condition rules out attempts to evade the consequences of actions for self-protection. In some cases, it can require actions to promote social change in line with one's moral conviction. The second, a *ceteris paribus* "dialogic condition," requires a willingness to communicate one's conviction to others and "engage them in reasoned deliberation about its merits."[188] Brownlee maintains that "our deepest commitments come with non-evasive, dialogic efforts."[189]

Christopher Cowley argues that the communicative principle of conscientiousness does not provide a reliable measure of the sincerity or depth of objectors' beliefs.[190] He focuses on the nonevasive condition and claims that objectors might fail to participate in public protests because they are not extroverted or confrontational or because they believe such actions are pointless and not because they lack sincere and deeply held moral convictions. There are several additional reasons that can explain a failure to satisfy the nonevasive and/or dialogic conditions – none of which implies that objectors' underlying moral beliefs are not sincere or among their "deepest commitments." Objectors may be unwilling to risk penalties and sanctions (e.g., legal liability, loss of license, employment, or hospital privileges) because of the expected impact on dependent family members whom they believe they have a moral obligation to protect. Alternatively, an unwillingness to risk penalties and sanctions can signal a lack of courage rather than a lack of moral commitment. Objectors might be reluctant to engage in dialogue because they are shy, nonassertive, or easily intimidated. Even if these traits are considered flaws in their moral character, it would not follow that the moral beliefs that ground their objections are not sincere or deeply held. Objectors may also be reluctant to engage in dialogue because they believe they lack relevant linguistic and cognitive skills or because they believe that attempting to engage in fruitful dialogue with individuals who do not share one's values is futile, frustrating, aggravating, annoying, unproductive, and ultimately a waste of time. Especially when objections are based on physicians' religious beliefs, they might be reluctant to subject what to them are deeply personal matters of faith to critical public scrutiny. In such cases, it can be disputed that an unwillingness to satisfy the dialogic condition is a sign that physicians' convictions are not among their "deepest." Physicians might fail to satisfy the dialogic condition when they communicate their refusals to patients because they believe that it is inappropriate to communicate moral disapproval to patients or to engage in what might (rightly or wrongly) be perceived as "preaching" or "badgering." Finally, objectors might believe, contrary to Brownlee, that satisfying the dialogic condition and challenging the values and moral beliefs of others is incompatible with respect for their agency and dignity. Even if Brownlee is correct, and that belief is mistaken, it does not follow that the beliefs that ground objectors' refusals are not sincere and deeply held.

A stated aim of Brownlee's analysis is to advocate for civil disobedience. Specifically, she challenges what she refers to as the "standard liberal" comparison of conscientious objection and civil disobedience: "[P]rivate, non-communicative acts of so-called 'conscientious objection' are more conscientious than suitably constrained communicative acts of disobedience such as civil disobedience ... I reverse the standard liberal picture and show that civil disobedience is more conscientious than personal disobedience in virtue of its constrained, communicative, and non-evasive properties."[191] Suppose, for the sake of argument, that we accept the claim that acts of civil disobedience are more conscientious than acts of conscientious objection. It can still be maintained that acts of conscientious objection that do not satisfy the communicative principle can be *sufficiently conscientious* to provide a *pro tanto* reason to accommodate objectors. For example, it can be maintained that objections can be sufficiently conscientious if they are genuine or based on core moral beliefs.

Compatibilists who acknowledge the importance of genuineness disagree about whether objectors should be required to *demonstrate* that their beliefs are genuine. Meyers and Woods are staunch advocates of such a requirement.[192] They support it by citing cases in which physicians who requested exemptions offered in conscience clauses did not have moral objections. Some objections were based on financial or aesthetic reasons. By contrast, Cowley argues that it is unnecessary to require objectors to demonstrate that their beliefs are genuine. He maintains that "while it is clear why a draftee would lie to conceal his non-moral reluctance, it is less clear what sort of non-moral reluctance a doctor could have."[193] Consequently, he claims, the number of objectors who feign moral opposition to abortion is not high enough to justify the costs associated with tribunals. Cowley qualifies his argument with two caveats. First, it applies specifically to conscientious objection to abortion in the United Kingdom. Second, it assumes physicians' refusals will not impede patients' convenient access to abortion.

Card challenges Cowley's argument.[194] He accuses Cowley of a "failure of imagination" and offers several reasons why physicians would use conscientious objection "as cover for a refusal based on non-moral reasons."[195] Insofar as the disagreement between Card and Cowley is about facts (i.e., how many physicians feign moral objection to abortion and the cost of assessing genuineness), its resolution requires empirical evidence. However, the disagreement is only partially about facts. It is also about the aim of assessing genuineness. If it is only to protect access to abortion, Cowley assumes that access can be protected more directly in the United Kingdom by the National Health Service. This suggests the following restatement of his conclusion: if an assessment of genuineness is not needed to protect access, it is unnecessary.

However, even when access is not at issue, there might be a reason to assess genuineness. For example, Card claims that "thoughtful individuals should not wish to grant such protection [accommodation] to any refusals in medicine except those founded upon core moral beliefs sincerely held by the individual."[196] It still is necessary to determine whether the frequency of requests for accommodation that are not genuine justifies the costs and burdens of assessing genuineness. In addition, some compatibilists have expressed doubts about the ability to reliably determine whether objections are genuine. For example, Cowley is skeptical about whether the interdisciplinary review boards that Meyers and Woods propose would have the required ability. The challenge of reliably assessing objectors' beliefs will be addressed more fully in Section 4.2.

4.2 Justifying Reasons

Compatibilists disagree about whether, to qualify for accommodation, objectors should be required to provide justifying reasons. As indicated in Section 3.3.3, Fernandez Lynch does not accept this requirement. Instead, she endorses what she refers to as "deep self-reflection."[197] Its function is twofold: (1) to determine whether objections are based on physicians' core moral beliefs and whether providing the service will compromise their moral integrity; (2) to ensure that their objections are based on "factually correct information."[198] Self-reflection is said to be a professional duty that is not legally enforceable. Notably, there is no belief-related requirement beyond self-reflection. Objectors are not required to publicly communicate their reasons or subject them to assessment by others (e.g., medical licensing boards, department heads, or ethics committees).

However, Fernandez Lynch claims that there is a "compelling argument" for encouraging objectors to share with their patients "the reasons that linger after deep self-reflection" – adding that it must be "in a respectful manner."[199] She maintains that sharing reasons is a means of "exposing patients to different ideas about the service in question."[200] Since patients can encounter these ideas from other sources, explaining their reasons for objecting "may not rise to the level of an actual obligation, but at the very least, it should be tolerated."[201]

In response, it can be objected that refusing requests for medical services is not an appropriate context for attempting to expand patients' moral horizons. Although physicians may intend to respect patients' differing views, there is a risk that patients will perceive that they are being morally judged, and they may feel insulted, disrespected, or demeaned. Moreover, patients who need a medical service might experience heightened levels of anxiety and can be especially vulnerable. In addition, in view of the power and knowledge differential between patients and physicians, there is a risk that patients will be intimidated by physicians who explain their moral objections. As observed previously, McLeod claims that disrespect and intimidation can be especially problematic in the context of reproductive health care due to social stigma. Fernandez Lynch maintains that there is an important difference between "moralizing condemnation or proselytizing" and "a clear exposition of the grounds for a physician's refusal."[202] However, due to the aforementioned factors, the distinction may be difficult to maintain in practice.

Compatibilists who require objectors to explain their justifying reasons face a substantial challenge: to specify justifiable criteria for assessing reasons that are clear and unambiguous. If criteria do not meet these conditions, there is a danger that assessments will be overly subjective and will be influenced by the beliefs and biases of reviewers. Thus, there is a risk that reviews will undermine the goal of providing objectors with moral space in which to practice medicine in accordance with *their* moral commitments.

Morten Magelssen's proposed assessment standard provides an example of criteria that do not meet this challenge.[203] His criteria require objectors to offer "well thought-through, detailed and plausible reasons."[204] Objections lack a plausible rationale if they are based on "erroneous factual premises."[205] This identifies one necessary condition of plausibility for fact-based beliefs – they are plausible only if they are not erroneous. But no standard is provided for determining whether a belief is erroneous. What evidence is required to determine that a fact-based belief is erroneous? What distinguishes erroneous from (highly) improbable beliefs? Is the burden of proof on the reviewer to provide sufficient evidence to warrant a judgment that the belief is erroneous? Or is the burden of proof on the objector to demonstrate that the belief is not erroneous?

Are all fact-based beliefs that are not erroneous plausible? Absent defensible answers to these and other questions, identifying erroneous factual premises can be overly subjective and improperly influenced by reviewers' biases.

Magelssen maintains that a necessary condition of plausibility in relation to a moral or religious belief is that "it fits into a coherent world view."[206] At first sight, this may seem to be an easily satisfiable standard that does not allow reviewers' values and beliefs to significantly influence judgments about the plausibility of objectors' reasons. However, without a clear and unambiguous criterion for determining whether beliefs fit into a "coherent world view," there is a risk that – intentionally or unintentionally – reviewers' beliefs and values will improperly affect plausibility assessments. The risk increases when Magelssen suggests an additional necessary condition: moral and religious beliefs are plausible only if they are not "incompatible with any *plausible* world view" (emphasis added).[207]

Robert Card has been a steadfast advocate of a requirement that objectors provide justifying reasons that are subjected to review and assessment. Over time, he has revised and more explicitly specified his proposed criteria for assessing justifying reasons. Examining changes in his proposed criteria over time illustrates the challenge facing compatibilists who propose a requirement that objectors offer satisfactory justifying reasons.

In a 2007 article, Card maintains that objectors' beliefs must be "reasonable" and should be evaluated with respect to their "justifiability."[208] Notably, Card provides no explicit criteria for determining whether objectors' reasons are "reasonable" or "justified." Instead, he provides examples of reasons that he claims fail to satisfy the requirements. In one case, an objector's reason for refusing to provide EC is based on the belief that it can have the effect of destroying fertilized ova. As the following statements indicate, Card acknowledges that when his article was published, the absence of this postfertilization effect had not been definitively established:

> [I]t is possible that EC may interfere with the transport of the embryo to the uterus or inhibit its implantation into the endometrium ... A review of the literature suggests that there is no solid reason to believe that hormonal EC works in either the former or latter manner ... ; recent scientific evidence ... suggests that hormonal EC does not have postfertilization effects (citations deleted).[209]

Card fails to provide an unambiguous and defensible general standard for determining whether empirical beliefs are unreasonable. Is an empirical belief unreasonable if: there is *no* supporting evidence; there is *too little* supporting evidence; there is *overwhelming* disconfirming evidence; confirming evidence is *insufficient* to outweigh disconfirming evidence? "To little," "overwhelming," and "insufficient" require specification to prevent overly subjective and improperly biased assessments of objectors' reasons. In addition, Card assumes without justification that objectors have the burden of demonstrating that their beliefs are reasonable. Why is the burden not on reviewers to demonstrate that objectors' beliefs are not reasonable and their justifications unsatisfactory?

Card considers the following "zero probability argument" that objectors to EC might offer, and he claims it is another instance of unreasonableness: "persons should not perform an action unless it is true that there is a zero probability that their action (or their contribution to an action) will issue in immoral results."[210] In response, it can be claimed that this is a straw person argument – an argument that no one is likely to make. To be sure, probability arguments are common, but the claim typically is that the probability that an action will have a wrongful outcome meets a minimal threshold condition above zero to warrant refusing to perform it. Is there a general threshold of reasonableness, or is it context dependent? Are agents' probability thresholds justifiably influenced by their perception of the gravity of the moral wrong at issue? These are among the relevant questions that Card does not address.

Card also applies the reasonableness standard to an objection to contraception based on the belief that "intercourse is ethically acceptable only if the goal is procreation."[211] He claims that this belief is unreasonable because "it is inconsistent with the compelling fundamental idea that adults possess a moral reproductive right founded in autonomy."[212] This response serves as a warning that insufficiently specified review criteria such as "unreasonable" can fail to filter out the influence of reviewers' values and ethical beliefs.

In response to Card's requirement that objectors provide justifying reasons, Jason Marsh claims that applying this requirement to nonempirical (e.g., moral and religious) beliefs gives rise to an epistemic challenge: specifying a standard of success that is neither too easy nor too hard.[213] If it is too hard, few, if any, physicians will be able to satisfy it, and the goals of accommodating conscientious objection will be thwarted. If it is too easy, it may be pointless because it will rule out few, if any, requests for accommodation.

Marsh's proposed solution to this alleged epistemic problem is to tailor the strength of the standard to address a *practical problem*: how to protect access. Specifically, how to ensure that accommodating physicians who object to a medical service will not significantly reduce the availability of the service. He proposes the following criterion for the strength of the standard for assessing justifying reasons as well as genuineness:

> in places where people are less likely to object, we should make objecting fairly easy (whether in the form of an easy reason-giving requirement, an easy genuineness requirement, or by having neither requirement). By contrast, in

places where many medical professionals are regularly objecting to treating patients, we need to do something about this. Perhaps one solution is to have would-be objectors defend themselves, while intentionally holding them, qua objectors or doctors, to high standards of rationality, standards that we would not hold them to in another context, qua persons.[214]

In response, it can be objected that Marsh's proposal risks promoting misunderstanding on the part of objectors about the aim of assessing their reasons. Whereas they might believe that the aim is to ascertain whether they can provide a reasonable justification for their objection, the actual primary aim is to protect access. Insofar as the aim is to protect access, transparency requires the implementation of a review mechanism with a publicly stated purpose of ensuring that accommodating physicians who object to providing a medical service will not significantly reduce the availability of that service. Jonathan Hughes offers one possible model for such a mechanism: review boards to assess physicians' requests for accommodation.[215] Rather than assessing an applicant's reasons, the primary function of a review board would be to ensure that a physician's refusal to provide a medical service will not reduce their patients' access to it. Doctors would be "required to submit for examination by a tribunal an explanation of how patients will be able to access the services from which the doctor intends to withdraw."[216]

In addition to increased transparency, an advantage of review boards along the lines proposed by Hughes is reducing the risk of insulting and demeaning applicants who are denied accommodation. If objectors are informed that a request for accommodation is denied to protect patient access, the denial is based on *professional norms* and *justice*. On the other hand, if objectors are told that a request for accommodation has been denied because their beliefs are not sufficiently reasonable, the denial is based on a judgment about *objectors* and *their beliefs*. Arguably, however, a major limitation of Hughes' proposal is its lack of practicability.

In an article in which he addresses Marsh's critique, Card states that he will defend the position that he refers to as the "Reasonability View" by addressing Marsh's criticisms, and that he will "further develop the reason-giving requirement [Marsh's label for Card's requirement that objectors' reasons must be reasonable] by outlining some of the primary criteria it uses to evaluate conscientious objections in medicine."[217] As he understands it, the Reasonability View is not limited to an assessment of an objector's reasons: "Reasonability . . . has to do not only with the intrinsic reasonability of beliefs supporting the claim, but also with the proper relative weight these competing considerations should be given in comparison with the professional's duties of care to the patient."[218] Assessing reasonability introduces another challenge: specifying justifiable, clear, and unambiguous criteria for assigning "weights" to competing values and interests.

Card does not offer any additional specification of the reason-giving requirement in relation to moral and metaphysical beliefs. Instead, he assigns this task to medical conscientious objector review (MCOR) boards without providing criteria for their reviews of the reasonableness of moral and metaphysical beliefs. He only proposes three general belief-related criteria: grounding beliefs must be "genuine" and "consonant with relevant empirical data," and must not be based on "discriminatory beliefs."[219] He provides no specification of the consonance requirement. Is it satisfied if/only if:

(1) The preponderance of evidence supports the objectors' beliefs; if so, what is needed for a *preponderance*?
(2) There is more evidence for the belief than against the belief; and if so, how much more?
(3) Relevant empirical evidence does not disconfirm the belief; and if so, what is required to disconfirm a belief?
(4) Relevant evidence justifies concluding that it is more likely than not that the belief is true/justified; and if so, when does relevant evidence satisfy this condition?

In subsequent publications, Card offers little additional specification of the proposed evaluation criteria that have been examined so far. He does provide several examples of empirical beliefs that do and do not satisfy the consonance condition in his 2020 book, *A New Theory of Conscientious Objection in Medicine*,[220] but no general standard is offered for assessing objectors' justifications. However, in a 2017 article,[221] he adds an explicit "public reason" requirement which he elaborates in subsequent publications.[222] This requirement serves as a condition of reasonable groundings of beliefs, and objectors' justifications must satisfy it. The primary question for reviewers is whether a justification is based on *public reason* – not whether it is convincing, plausible, logically sound, supported by good reasons, and so forth. Thus, it might be claimed that the public reason requirement eliminates or significantly reduces the concern that an insufficiently specified reasonability requirement risks introducing unacceptable subjectivity and bias into reviewers' assessments of objectors' reasons and justifications.

Card cites John Rawls' explanation of the "ideal of public reason:" "This ideal is that citizens are to conduct their public political discussions of constitutional essentials and matters of basic justice within the framework of what each sincerely regards as a reasonable political conception of justice, a conception that expresses political values that others as free and equal might also reasonably be expected reasonably to endorse."[223] As Rawls understands it, the ideal of public reason is said to impose a constraint that applies specifically to *constitutional essentials* and *matters of basic justice*. Card offers the following explanation of these concepts: "By constitutional essentials, Rawls means political rights and liberties one might want enshrined in a constitution, and by matters of basic justice, Rawls means matters that 'relate to the basic structure of society and so would concern questions of basic economic and social justice and other things not covered by a constitution'."[224]

It is questionable whether objectors' grounding beliefs fall within the scope of Rawls' public reason requirement. They are not attempting to justify enshrining specified political rights and liberties in a constitution; nor are they attempting to justify a conception of basic economic rights and liberties. In response, Card cites the example of conscientious objection in reproductive health to make the case that objectors' beliefs fall within the scope of the public reason requirement:

> [R]eproductive rights vis à vis access to abortion has been noted by the US Supreme Court to be an issue of social justice, and the effects of legalized access to abortion have been identified by the Court as having a positive effect on women's equality and political rights in this country ... [S]ystematically deny[ing] women access to reproductive services via conscientious objection ... goes against the idea of women as free and equal citizens. Relating to such matters, then, on a Rawlsian approach such providers must not solely appeal to their personal, comprehensive doctrines in their refusals of care within the institutional structure of medicine but must appeal to public reasons – those that are consistent with a reasonable public conception of justice.[225]

Notably, Card fails to distinguish between what might be termed a "meta question" about an institutional framework of rules regulating conscientious objection in medicine, on the one hand, and a criterion for assessing objectors' reasons for refusing to provide medical services, on the other hand. His explanation of a "Rawlsian approach" suggests that it is the former, not the latter, that is subject to a public reason constraint. Institutional rules that satisfy the public reason condition might not require individual objectors to satisfy it. At most, one might claim that whether objectors' reasons are subject to a public reason condition is an issue that itself is subject to that condition.

In response to the proposed public reason requirement, Nir Ben-Moshe, in a 2019 article, suggests that it is too demanding. He claims that "it is very unlikely that most medical professionals would be able to state their objections in terms of public reasons rather than in terms of their own idiosyncratic reasons."[226] Arguably, any stringent criterion risks setting the bar so high that objectors would rarely qualify for accommodation. Objectors can have sincere and deeply held self-defining core moral convictions and yet lack the critical thinking skills that would enable them to provide a satisfactory justification of their grounding reasons; or they might opt to shield core convictions, especially if they are faith-based, from public scrutiny. If objections are not based on disqualifying reasons such as those identified earlier, it is unclear why an inability (or unwillingness) to provide a satisfactory justification to reviewers should disqualify physicians from being considered for accommodation.

Card provides a reason: "If one wonders why individual medical providers need to supply justifications for conscientious exemptions, my answer is that fundamental respect to others as sensible, rational creatures and as moral agents requires that we do so. Reasons are what we owe to humanity."[227] In response, it can be maintained that the principle of respect for persons also requires respect for *objectors* as sensible, rational creatures and as moral agents; and it can be claimed that it is incompatible with this principle to challenge objectors' justifications of their deeply held moral and religious beliefs. Objectors might perceive such challenges as insulting or disrespectful – especially when the burden of proof is on them to demonstrate that their justifications are satisfactory. Arguably, it would be more respectful if the burden of proof were on reviewers to demonstrate that objectors' justifications are unsatisfactory. Additionally, it can be claimed that reviews of objectors' justifications are respectful only if justifications are assessed by criteria that are not improperly subjective or influenced by reviewers' beliefs and values.

4.3 Two Approaches That Do Not Require Objectors to Offer Justifying Reasons

In a 2021 article, Ben-Moshe proposes an alternative approach to justification which, he maintains, avoids requiring objectors to provide justifying reasons.[228] He proposes an "Uber Conscientious Objection in Medicine Committee" (UCOM Committee) that will rely exclusively on public reasons to identify *types of conscientious objections* that are justified. According to Ben-Moshe, identifying types of conscientious objections that do and do not qualify for accommodation eliminates the need to assess individual objectors' reasons.

Conscientious objection types are identified by the target of the objection. Ben-Moshe offers only one specific example: objections to abortion. This suggests that types of conscientious objections can be identified by medical procedures or services (e.g., objections to abortion, EC, MAID, or palliative sedation to unconsciousness). However, other types of conscientious objections that the committee might subject to a public reason assessment include objections to providing services to certain classes of patients (e.g., Black, Muslim, and LGBTQ patients). If the UCOM Committee determines that a public reason justification can be given for a specified type of conscientious objection, individual providers are not required to offer a public justification. If the committee determines that a public reason justification cannot be given for a specific type of conscientious objection (e.g., an objection to treating LGBTQ patients), no objections of this type are justified. Insofar as Ben-Moshe's approach to justification does not require an assessment of individuals' reasons, it avoids the risk of requiring cognitive skills that are excessively demanding.

Ben-Moshe considers the following objection: "one could insist that hearing out the objecting physician is important, since we should hear her own reasons for the objection."[229] In response, he states "given my emphasis on public reason, there is no special importance to hearing out the medical physician's own personal justifications for her conscientious objection, nor should we expect her to state such an objection in general terms."[230]

Doug McConnell and Card offer a reason for considering objectors' own personal justifications.[231] These authors are concerned that if objectors' reasons are not subject to public review, there is a danger that "objections with discriminatory, self-interested, arbitrary, empirically inaccurate, normatively bizarre and insincere grounds" will be accommodated.[232] To be sure, a UCOM Committee should exclude types of objections that can only be justified on such grounds. However, nothing will prevent individual providers from objecting to medical services for which there are permissible types of objections for inappropriate or unacceptable reasons; and McConnell and Card can maintain that objections based on inappropriate or unacceptable reasons – regardless of whether the objection type has received UCOM Committee approval – should not be accommodated. They can argue that since a UCOM Committee can determine only whether a *type* of conscientious objection is justifiable, it cannot determine whether the *provider's* objection is justified because a provider's objection is justified only if the provider's reasons satisfy a reasonableness condition.

Ben-Moshe assumes that a UCOM Committee should restrict justifiable types of objections to those that can be given a public reason justification. But one can ask, why should conscientious objections to a specified medical service provide a *pro tanto* reason for accommodation only if they satisfy the public reason constraint? Might the choice of assessment criteria be a task that is best left to a Meta-UCOM Committee to decide?

In his earlier 2019 article, Ben-Moshe offers another approach that does not require objectors to provide *their* actual reasons. What matters, he claims, is whether claims of conscience can be justified from the perspective of an impartial spectator. He maintains that "the reasonableness of a conscientious objection is a function of deliberation from the standpoint of an impartial spectator and not from the individual physician's own point of view."[233] Claims of conscience that are justifiable from the former perspective are said to be "true, or at least [to] approximate moral truth to the greatest degree possible for creatures like us, and should thus be respected."[234] Claims of conscience are said to be "legitimate" if and only if they are made from that perspective.

Ben-Moshe admits that there are "complicated cases" for which an impartial spectator analysis alone cannot provide a decisive answer. Two that he identifies are conscientious objections to first trimester abortion and MAID. In such cases, he asserts, without any argument, that an impartial spectator would invoke the principle of epistemic modesty and conclude that objecting physicians' claims of conscience are legitimate: "[T]he physician's claim of conscience, although not conclusively true, is also justified, because it is a judgment made from the standpoint of an impartial spectator and thus approximates moral truth to the greatest degree possible."[235]

Ben-Moshe maintains that claims of conscience are legitimate only if *objectors themselves* use the impartial spectator test to assess their claims of conscience: "[A] medical professional cannot be said to have formulated a legitimate conscientious objection unless they have made a good faith attempt to adopt the standpoint of an impartial spectator, and so we should only accept an appeal to conscience if we have reason to believe that the objector has made such an attempt."[236] Thus, according to Ben-Moshe, although objectors are not required to disclose and justify their *personal moral convictions*, they are required to determine whether their claims of conscience are justifiable from the standpoint of an impartial observer. This requirement seems odd. To see why, suppose that a physician conscientiously objects to providing medical service x, and impartial spectator reasoning confirms that an objection to x is justifiable. According to Ben-Moshe, it would follow that the objector's belief that providing x is morally wrong approximates moral truth to the greatest degree possible. Arguably, if that belief approximates moral truth to the greatest degree possible, accommodation should not be contingent on requiring the objector to demonstrate an ability to offer a justification from an impartial observer standpoint. Suppose the objector's reasoning was based on utilitarian or Kantian reasoning, and they are incapable of providing, or refuse to provide, an impartial observer justification. Arguably, it would be wrong to require them to provide x.

Ben-Moshe claims that assessing the *genuineness* of the objection is another function of the requirement that objectors should justify their refusals from the standpoint of an impartial spectator: "[R]ather than trying to ascertain whether the objector sincerely holds the idiosyncratic beliefs on which her objection is initially based, genuineness could be ascertained by determining whether the objector has in fact gone through the impartial spectator procedure."[237] This claim can be challenged. An objector's ability to provide an impartial spectator justification does not warrant a conclusion about genuineness. A philosopher or an Artificial Intelligence (AI) chatbot might be able to provide impartial spectator justifications of views without accepting them.

Ben-Moshe's approach is subject to several additional challenges. First, it is based on a controversial and contested conception of truth and ethical justification (an impartial spectator conception).[238] Second, a requirement that claims of conscience are legitimate only if they "are true, or at least approximate moral truth to the greatest degree possible for creatures like us" is incompatible with two frequently cited goals of accommodation: (1) giving objectors moral space in which to practice medicine without going against their moral convictions; and (2) promoting tolerance of moral diversity. Third, insofar as objections are based on beliefs that are true, or at least approximate moral truth to the greatest degree possible for creatures like us, it is arguable that rather than having permission to refuse, objectors – and all physicians – have a *moral obligation* to refuse.

5 Accommodation and Conscientious Provision

Up to this point, the focus has been on conscientious *objection*. In this section, the focus will shift to conscientious *provision*. As explained in Section 2.2, whereas conscientious objection involves a refusal to provide legally and institutionally permitted medical services that are contrary to a physician's moral convictions, conscientious provision occurs when physicians (conscientious providers) offer legally or institutionally prohibited medical services because they believe they have a moral and/or professional obligation to offer them.

There is substantial asymmetry in law and public and institutional policy between the response to conscientious objection and provision.[239] Whereas conscientious objectors (physicians with negative conscience claims) often receive (conditional) accommodation, physicians who believe they have an obligation to provide prohibited services (physicians with positive conscience claims) typically are not accommodated. For example, conscience clauses offer legal protections to OB–GYNs in the United States who conscientiously object to participating in pregnancy termination. Protections vary by state, but can include immunity from legal liability, employment-related penalties, and loss of license to practice medicine. By contrast, states that restrict or prohibit abortion do not offer any exemptions to OB–GYNs who believe that denying an abortion to a patient is contrary to their obligation to promote the health and well-being of their patients.[240] Similarly, states that ban or restrict providing gender-affirming care to minors do not provide exemptions for pediatricians who believe they have an obligation to provide such care – with parental consent – when it will protect the health and well-being of patients. Is this asymmetry justified? This question is especially pertinent since it can be maintained that common rationales for accommodating conscientious objectors (Section 3.1) apply as well to conscientious providers.[241]

An obvious strategy to justify asymmetry is to argue that there are relevant differences. Candidates include: (1) an alleged ethical difference in types of duties – negative and positive duties – that corresponds to the difference between conscientious objection and conscientious provision;[242] (2) an alleged ethical difference between compelling someone to act contrary to their moral convictions and prohibiting them from acting in accordance with those convictions;[243] (3) an alleged difference in the impact of accommodation on other health professionals, institutions, and society;[244] and (4) an alleged difference in whether lawbreaking is condoned and whether state interests are thwarted.[245]

5.1 Negative versus Positive Duties

It is not uncommon to distinguish between two types of duties – negative and positive. Several definitions have been offered. Some focus on a distinction between omissions and acts. For example, according to Marcus Singer, "A negative duty is a duty not to do something, a duty of omission. A positive duty is a duty to do something and cannot be fulfilled by inaction."[246] Jan Narveson offers a similar account: "A positive duty is a duty to do something, whereas a negative duty is a duty ('merely') to refrain from doing something."[247] Other definitions include a reference to harm and harm prevention. For example, according to H. M. Malm, negative duties are "duties not to cause harm," and positive duties are "duties to prevent harm."[248] Similarly, Raymond Belliotti defines negative duties as duties to "refrain from harming or injuring others" and positive duties as duties to "render assistance to those in distress."[249] By contrast, Nancy Davis limits negative duties to duties to refrain from harmful acts of commission and understands positive duties as duties to perform beneficial acts of commission. Negative duties are said to be "duties not to actively harm," and positive duties are said to be "duties to actively benefit."[250] The act–omission distinction will be used for the purposes of this discussion.

Typically, regardless of the definition, it is assumed that compared to positive duties, negative duties are more stringent or demanding and their violation is morally worse. This understanding of the moral difference between the two types of duties will be referred to as the "moral asymmetry principle" (MAP). It can be used to generate a "moral asymmetry argument" (MAA).

MAA: Whereas conscientious objectors who claim to have a duty to refuse to provide medical services are appealing to a negative duty; conscientious providers who claim to have a duty to provide medical services are appealing to a positive duty. MAP implies that compared to accommodating conscientious providers, accommodating conscientious objectors exempts physicians from duties that are more stringent and the violation of which is morally worse. Therefore, conscientious objectors have a stronger moral claim to accommodation than conscientious providers.

The underlying premise, MAP, can be challenged. Consider two cases.

Case 1: Konstantin witnesses a boating accident. He is unable to rescue the survivors himself, but he could call the coast guard on his cell phone. Had he done so, the coast guard would have been able to rescue the survivors. Konstantin had a positive duty to call the coast guard, but he decided not to because he would have incurred a roaming charge of $1.50. The survivors died.

Case 2: On her way home, carrying a bag of tomatoes, Penelope walks by a protest. She disagrees with the politics of the protestors and violates a negative duty by throwing tomatoes at them.

Unquestionably, Konstantin's violation of his positive duty is morally (much) worse than Penelope's violation of her negative duty.

In response, it might be suggested that a comparison of the two types of duties needs to compare *corresponding* negative and positive duties. For example, a negative duty corresponding to the positive duty in Case 1 might be a duty not to kill. Consider Case 3.

Case 3: Gustav violates a negative duty by deliberately killing the survivors of a boating accident.

Arguably, Gustav's violation of the negative duty not to deliberately kill innocent persons is morally worse than Konstantin's positive duty to call the coast guard. But consider Cases 4 and 5.

Case 4: Walter violates a negative duty by unintentionally but negligently killing the survivors of a boating accident.

Case 5: Maria violates a positive duty by deliberately failing to throw a life preserver to her husband after their sailboat capsized due to a sudden violent wind burst. She wants him to die because she wants to marry Jonah, with whom she has had an affair for over a month.

It is not implausible to claim that Maria's violation of her positive duty is morally worse than Walter's violation of his negative duty.

Cases 4 and 5 suggest that a more nuanced formulation of the comparison of the two types of duties is required to account for possible morally significant differences in motive, intention, burdensomeness, and so forth. MAP* addresses this concern by including an "all other things being equal" qualifier:

MAP*: All other things being equal, violations of negative duties are morally worse than violations of corresponding positive duties.

For the sake of argument, let us accept MAP* and apply it to Case 6.

Case 6: Marcela Simonetti is a pregnant ICU patient who is in a permanent vegetative state. Her living will unambiguously indicates that she does not want life-sustaining treatment in her current clinical condition. Her husband Alfred was with her when she discussed her living will with her OB–GYN three months after learning that she was pregnant. At that meeting, she insisted that she wanted her living will to be honored even if it violated a state law restricting the implementation of the living wills of pregnant patients. "Keeping me alive just to deliver a baby," Ms. Simonetti insisted, "would treat me as nothing more than a baby-making and incubating machine. It would be an insult to my dignity. It also would violate my autonomy and my right to decide what happens in and to my body. I don't want to give birth to a motherless child or burden my husband with the responsibility of being a single parent." When Dr. Birnbaum, the ICU attending, discusses Ms. Simonetti's advance directive with her husband, Alfred recounts Marcela's discussions with her OB–GYN. Dr. Birnbaum believes she has a moral obligation to honor Ms. Simonetti's advance directive. The state law that prohibits implementing advance directives of pregnant patients like Ms. Simonetti does not offer any accommodation to physicians like Dr. Birnbaum who believe they have a moral obligation to implement such directives. However, it offers (qualified) accommodation to physicians like Dr. Chang who believe they have a moral obligation to refuse to implement an advance directive.

It might be questioned whether (1) the relevant duties in Case 6 can be classified as negative (Dr. Chang) and positive (Dr. Birnbaum); (2) they are corresponding duties; and (3) all other things are equal. However, for the sake of analysis, let us assume that each of these three conditions is satisfied. For several reasons, MAP* does not provide a justification for accommodating conscientious objectors like Dr. Chang but not accommodating conscientious providers like Dr. Birnbaum.

First, whereas MAP* is about *violations* of negative and positive duties and *moral wrongs*, conscientious objection and provision are about *perceived* duties and *perceived* moral wrongs. A difference in *perceived duties* and *perceived moral wrongs* distinguishes the two physicians. Dr. Chang *believes* he has a duty to refuse to honor living wills and that implementing them is a moral wrong. Dr. Birnbaum *believes* that she has a duty to implement living wills like Ms. Simonetti's and that failing to do so is morally wrong.

Second, putting aside the difference between perceived and actual moral wrongness, insofar as MAP* only *compares* moral wrongs associated with violations of negative and positive duties, it cannot support selectively accommodating Dr. Chang or conscientious objectors generally. At most, it might be used to prioritize or assign moral weights to claims for accommodation corresponding to the (perceived) moral wrongness associated with violations of the (perceived) duties at issue. To deny accommodation to conscientious providers like Dr. Birnbaum and grant accommodation to conscientious objectors like Dr. Chang would require arguing that only the latter can reach the threshold of (perceived) wrongness that merits accommodation.

Finally, if an aim of accommodation is to enable physicians to practice medicine without compromising their moral integrity, MAP* does not provide relevant guidance. Whether their moral integrity is at stake is a function of their core moral beliefs. Absent information about the nature and depth of their moral beliefs, it is unwarranted to assume that whereas implementing Ms. Simonetti's advance directive as well as those of other patients would compromise Dr. Chang's moral integrity, failing to implement advance directives for patients like Ms. Simonetti would not compromise Dr. Birnbaum's moral integrity. Arguably, it is unwarranted to assume that whereas refusing to accommodate conscientious refusals can rise to the level of threatening physicians' moral integrity, refusing to accommodate conscientious providers cannot.[251]

Lisa Harris cites a passage from Carole Joffe's *Doctors of Conscience*[252] that offers a poignant example of conscientious providers who performed illegal abortions before *Roe* v. *Wade*:

> They did so with little to gain and much to lose, facing fines, imprisonment, and loss of medical license. They did so because the beliefs that mattered most to them compelled them to. They saw women die from self-induced abortions and abortions performed by unskilled providers. They understood safe abortion to be lifesaving. They believed their abortion provision honored "the dignity of humanity" and was the right – even righteous – thing to do. They performed abortions "for reasons of conscience."[253]

It is unimaginable that denying all abortion requests would not have compromised their moral integrity. A similar claim can be made about a physician's commitment to treating their transgender patients and who stated, "As a matter of conscience, I am called to do this work."[254]

5.2 Compelling versus Not Prohibiting

Dov Fox considers an argument in defense of asymmetry that is said to be based on a distinction between doing and allowing:

> [T]he distinction between doing and allowing runs deep in our moral and legal culture. A liberal society can prevent people from acting in all sorts of harmful ways, but rarely force them to act to avoid similar harm. Compelling religious sacraments seems crueler than prohibiting them, while making someone say something they deem false or wrong might be thought grimmer than preventing a person from speaking. On this view, forcing clinicians to provide care they morally oppose is worse than preventing them from supplying care their scruples command them to. Forced actions are more harmful than forced omissions, justifying greater protections for conscientious refusal than for conscientious provision.[255]

Fox does not directly challenge the doing/allowing distinction. Instead, he maintains that it has less weight in the context of health care: "Distinguishing doing from allowing assumes diminished significance in the medical domain. Conscientious refusers and providers owe similar duties to put their patients first."[256]

In response, it is unclear that the distinction between conscientious objection and provision corresponds to the doing/allowing distinction. A paradigm case of the latter in medicine is the distinction between killing (allegedly a doing) and allowing to die (allegedly an allowing). Conscientious objectors can have a moral objection to both, and conscientious providers can believe they have a moral obligation to honor competent patients' informed requests for both. In relation to abortion, conscientious objectors believe that providing abortions is morally wrong, and conscientious providers believe that not providing them is morally wrong. Their disagreement, unlike disagreements about killing and letting die, does not appear to be related to the doing/allowing distinction. Thus, it is questionable whether a justification of asymmetry can be based on that distinction.

There are two objections to the argument Fox considers that are unrelated to the doing/allowing distinction. First, it is misleading to claim that not accommodating objectors *compels* them to violate their moral convictions. Objectors have a choice – one suggested by incompatibilists that advocates of accommodation are likely to claim objectors should not be required to make – but a choice, nonetheless. They can choose another specialty, practice location, or profession.

Second, it is unclear whether one can generalize about harm. If a physician's moral integrity is at stake, it might not matter whether it is undermined by providing a medical service or failing to provide a medical service. There might be no significant difference in the amount of experienced moral harm. Even if there is a difference, as Fox suggests, the harm in both cases might be sufficient to warrant preventing both, and the difference might be insufficient to justify only preventing the lesser harm and offering conscientious providers *no protection*.[257]

5.3 Impact on Other Health Professionals, Institutions, and Society

The forgoing arguments for asymmetry focus on alleged differences in what is at stake for objectors and providers. However, some defenders of asymmetry argue that accommodating conscientious providers can be significantly more burdensome to other health professionals, institutions, and society. Abram Brummett claims that accommodating conscientious providers can compromise institutional values in a way and to an extent that accommodating conscientious objectors does not.[258] He uses Catholic hospitals and their prohibition of abortion to illustrate this claim. He maintains that accommodating conscientious providers who believe they have a duty to terminate pregnancies to protect patients' health and well-being would substantially compromise the hospital's values – its "conscience." Brummett contrasts this situation with conscientious objection in hospitals with a commitment to offering abortions whenever it is standard of care. According to Brummett, arrangements can be put into place to accommodate objectors without compromising the hospital's commitment to offering pregnancy terminations: "[E]ven if several clinicians [conscientious objectors] assert a negative claim of conscience, institutional values can remain upheld with clear communication and careful scheduling; if one clinician objects to providing a service, then another can step in. A hospital that provides abortion can often still provide abortion even if several clinicians at the hospital conscientiously object."[259]

Brummett draws a second contrast based on an alleged difference in the institutional resources that accommodation requires. The contrast relies on a distinction between positive and negative rights. Negative rights are rights to be left alone. They protect liberty and function as shields against interference by others. For example, understood exclusively as a negative right, the right to life protects individuals from being killed. By contrast, positive rights can require the assistance of others. Understood as a positive right, it can be maintained that the right to life entitles individuals to assistance and/or resources (e.g., food, shelter, and health care) when needed to keep them alive. Understanding conscientious providers' positive conscience claims as positive rights claims, Brummett maintains that accommodation requires making available to them the hospital resources needed to provide the medical services at issue. This is said to be a substantial burden to the institution and a violation of its "property right to use its resources as it sees fit."[260]

Brummett's defense of asymmetry can be challenged for several reasons. First, it is limited in scope. It is limited to conscientious provision in an institutional context, and one of his two arguments applies only to institutions that are said to have a "conscience" (i.e., a commitment to values). At most, then, he has shown that *in some contexts*, there can be distinctive reasons to deny accommodation to conscientious providers. The reasons are distinctive in the sense that they do not apply to conscientious objectors. Arguably, even if there are distinctive reasons to deny accommodation to conscientious providers in *some contexts*, absent empirical data about their frequency, it is unwarranted to selectively protect conscientious objectors in law and public policy.

Second, it can be objected that Brummett's assertion that the conscience claims of providers are positive rights claims is not generalizable. Dominic Wilkinson offers three counterexamples: conscientious providers in Catholic hospitals that do not permit physicians to write prescriptions for medical abortions, contraception, and MAID.[261] In such cases, Wilkinson maintains, conscientious providers can be understood to be claiming a negative right to not be prevented from acting. Assuming that patients are seen regardless of whether they receive the requested medications and external pharmacies supply them, Wilkinson argues, physicians would not be claiming a positive right to hospital resources. It might be objected that accommodating those conscientious providers requires the provision of *some* institutional resources (e.g., institutional facilities and prescription pads). However, even if this claim is not disputed, it is implausible to claim that, generally, providing those kinds of resources is an *excessive* burden on a hospital.

Third, Brummett's assertion that a hospital has a "property right to use its resources as it sees fit" can be challenged. Hospitals are licensed by governments and are subject to regulations that, among other things, can restrict their discretion over the use of resources. Hospitals in public health-care systems such as the National Health Service in the United Kingdom and the Veterans Health Administration in the United States are publicly funded; and private hospitals can receive government funding – either directly from grants or indirectly from tax exemptions. Government funding can come with mandates and constraints. Giubilini argues that constraints on health-care institutions, including religious hospitals, are ethically justified: "As monopoly providers of an essential good like healthcare, perhaps the most essential good in our societies, these institutions are subject to certain ethical constraints, and should be subject to certain regulatory constraints, regardless of whether they are public or private, religious or secular in nature."[262]

Fourth, Brummett's consideration of burdens focuses on the increased burdens to Catholic hospitals from accommodating conscientious providers.

Notably, however, denying them accommodation can increase the burdens experienced by *patients* due to a lack of timely access to legal and professionally accepted medical services.[263] Whereas accommodating conscientious objectors can impose burdens on patients, some bioethicists claim that accommodating conscientious providers can benefit patients; and they argue that this is an asymmetry that privileges accommodating conscientious providers.[264]

Fifth, it can be objected that Brummett significantly underestimates the burdens that can be associated with accommodating conscientious objectors.[265] Whether other providers can "step in" for objectors without imposing excessive burdens on medical staff and the institution is context dependent.[266] It can be influenced by several factors, including the number of staff members whose clinical competencies overlap with those of objectors; their current responsibilities and workloads; their willingness to provide the medical services in question; the number of health professionals within a service, unit, and the institution who request accommodation; and the frequency of such requests. In addition, reassigning responsibilities and implementing measures to accommodate objectors can be burdensome to department heads and administrators. Finally, financial resources may be required to hire more full- or part-time staff. Arguably, the burdensomeness of accommodation to institutions and the health professionals who practice in them is context dependent no matter whether it is in response to conscientious objectors or conscientious providers; and in both cases, a relevant question is whether expected burdens are excessive.[267] Dov Fox proposes "objector fees" to "defray the practical expenses that exemption incurs to the employer."[268] To avoid asymmetry, he also proposes fees to offset some of the costs of accommodating conscientious providers. The fairness of this proposal can be questioned insofar as it can tie accommodation to ability to pay.

Sixth, Brummett incorrectly assumes that accommodating conscientious objectors cannot compromise an institution's values.[269] Just as providing a medical service that is standard of care can be contrary to an institution's values or culture, refusing to provide a medical service that is standard of care can be contrary to the "culture" or values of a hospital or clinic. For example, Planned Parenthood clinics can have a commitment to providing a comprehensive range of family planning services, including abortion and contraception, and sharing this commitment can be a condition of practicing within the clinic.

Seventh, those who deny that institutions can have a conscience will reject Brummett's claim that, like individual clinicians, institutions can have a conscience that deserves protection.[270] If taken literally, it would be implausible to claim that institutions can have and exercise a conscience. Institutions do not appear to have the characteristics that would warrant ascribing those capacities to them. As George Annas observes, "Hospitals are corporations that have no natural personhood, and hence are incapable of having either 'moral' or 'ethical' objections to actions."[271]

To be sure, institutions are not living, conscious organisms. They lack awareness and do not have the capacity to think, form intentions, or feel good or bad. Moreover, in contrast to physicians, institutions cannot experience the effects of a loss of moral integrity, and they cannot experience guilt or suffer from injury to their identity. Nevertheless, claims can be advanced on behalf of health-care institutions that bear a family resemblance to conscience claims by individuals.[272] In some cases, a health-care institution's mission can be considered an analogue to the conscience of a health-care professional. As Kevin Wildes puts it: "[A]n institution can have a moral identity and conscience. A necessary condition for talking about institutional conscience is the moral identity of an institution. One way to explore this moral identity is to look at the mission of an institution."[273]

Although most, if not all, hospitals have mission statements, only some can plausibly claim to have genuine missions (i.e., a commitment to goals, values, and principles) that comprise a distinct identity and provide the basis for what might be considered analogues to conscience claims. Health-care institutions with a commitment to religious principles often have genuine missions, and a paradigm example is provided by Catholic hospitals in the United States that have a commitment to the Ethical and Religious Directives for Catholic Health Care Services.[274]

In response, suppose it is insisted that although hospitals can have a commitment to core ethical principles that comprise their institutional identity, it is nevertheless implausible to claim that they have a *conscience*. If Brummett's aim is to argue that hospitals can have a legitimate moral claim to protect their distinctive core values and identities, he need not assert that they have a conscience. It suffices to argue that they have a legitimate moral claim that should not be overlooked or discounted. However, acknowledging it to be a legitimate moral claim does not imply that hospitals' moral claims generally trump the legitimate claims of conscientious providers or objectors who practice within the institution.[275]

5.4 Condoning Lawbreaking and Thwarting State Interests

Another defense of asymmetry maintains that whereas accommodations for conscientious objectors only exempt them from providing legal services, accommodating conscientious providers gives them permission to break the law and condones lawbreaking.[276]

In response, it can be claimed that insofar as conscience clauses provide legal exemptions for conscientious providers, they are not breaking the law when they provide otherwise legally prohibited medical services.[277] For example, a state legislature enacts a law that prohibits offering gender-affirming care to anyone under the age of eighteen, and the law includes a conscience clause that exempts conscientious providers if they satisfy specified conditions. Physicians who satisfy those conditions are not violating the law when they provide gender-affirming care to adolescents. Of course, one can still ask whether an exemption for conscientious providers is justified.

Defenders of asymmetry can give another reason for limiting conscience clauses to conscientious objection. They can claim that in contrast to conscience clauses that shield conscientious objectors, those that shield conscientious providers threaten the state interests that the law in question aims to protect.[278] Consider again gender-affirming care for adolescents. Insofar as a state law that prohibits offering gender-affirming care to anyone under the age of eighteen is enacted to promote the state's interest in preventing adolescents from receiving gender-affirming care, a conscience clause that exempts conscientious providers would thwart that interest. By contrast, conscience clauses that permit conscientious objectors to refuse to provide medical services need not thwart a state's interest in making legal medical services accessible.

In response, it can be claimed that although it may be correct in principle that conscience clauses for conscientious objectors do not necessarily thwart a state objective to make legal medical services accessible, in practice they can pose significant barriers to access.[279] Since conscience clauses typically do not include conditions that protect patient access, it can be questioned whether patient access is a policy goal.

It has been objected that an aim of conscience clauses for conscientious providers would be to create a "back door" for changing restrictive laws by poking "enough holes in a blanket prohibition so that the exception becomes the rule."[280] In view of the absence of protections for patient access in conscience clauses for objectors and the ideological agenda they typically favor, it might be claimed that conscience clauses serve as a "back door" for substantially reducing the availability of specified medical services (e.g., abortion, emergency contraception, and MAID). Both types of back door objections shift the focus from accommodation to a policy question about access: To which medical services should patients have access?

As an alternative to exempting conscientious providers from all penalties and sanctions, it has been proposed that they should be able to offer affirmative defenses for specified legally prohibited services that can mitigate penalties and sanctions.[281] Depending on the medical service and the circumstances, mitigation can involve reductions in fines, not being subject to loss of license, no imprisonment, reduced sentences, and the like. Fox and Elizabeth Sepper limit this defense to legally prohibited medical services that are "clinically reasonable."[282] As Fox explains this standard, it "tracks the one that medical malpractice doctrine uses to determine deviations from acceptable care."[283] It "requires doctors to conform their conduct to what is 'reasonable to expect of a professional' in the relevant specialty 'given the state of medical knowledge' and patient specific facts that a physician is aware of, or should be."[284] The clinically reasonable standard disqualifies "treatments that are experimental, invalidated, or biologically implausible."[285] Fox admits that there are gray areas and close calls (e.g., puberty blockers for adolescents), but maintains there are clear cases of medical services that satisfy the standard (e.g., clinically indicated abortions and EC), and that do not meet it (e.g., conversion therapy and Ivermectin for COVID-19).

This mitigation approach is subject to three challenges. First, insofar as the rationales for accommodating conscientious objectors include sustaining a "dynamic profession,"[286] maintaining openness to moral progress, and acknowledging epistemic humility, offering mitigation only to conscientious providers who are committed to providing what is considered "clinically reasonable" (essentially standard of care) at a given time risks thwarting a similar objective in relation to conscientious provision. Second, it might be objected that the mitigation approach to conscientious provision retains unjustified asymmetry. Conscientious objectors enjoy a broad range of protections from legal liability. Yet, conscientious providers are not offered comparably strong protections. The justification for these different approaches to accommodation can be challenged. Third, it can be questioned whether mitigation adequately addresses what may well be an underlying objection to laws that prohibit the provision of medical services that are "clinically reasonable": the belief that such laws are unjustified. If this is an underlying objection, nothing short of repealing them would be sufficient.

6 Conclusion

Conscientious *objection* involves a refusal to provide legally and institutionally permitted medical services that are contrary to a physician's moral convictions. By contrast, conscientious *provision* occurs when physicians (conscientious providers) offer legally or institutionally prohibited medical services because they believe they have a moral and/or professional obligation to do so.

There is substantial agreement that conscientious refusals must be based on objectors' moral beliefs. Beyond that, there is a debate about requiring additional conditions, such as that the beliefs must be among the objectors' identity-conferring core moral beliefs. However, it is only when this additional condition is satisfied that enabling objectors to practice medicine without undermining their moral integrity can be a reason to accommodate.

One of the most hotly debated questions is whether conscientious objectors should be accommodated. A general aim of accommodation is to give objecting physicians moral space in which to practice medicine in accordance with their moral convictions. To ask whether physicians who conscientiously object should be accommodated is to ask whether they should be able to refuse to offer or provide medical services that are contrary to their moral convictions without facing sanctions or penalties, such as suspension, dismissal, loss of hospital privileges, censure, loss of medical license, or legal liability. There is general agreement that physicians are free to refuse to offer or provide medical services that are illegal, contrary to standard of care, or outside the scope of their clinical competence. Consequently, the issue of accommodation generally does not arise for such refusals. However, with respect to medical services that are legal, standard of care, and within the scope of a physician's clinical competency, there is considerable controversy about whether or when to accommodate conscientious objectors.

There are several *pro tanto* reasons for accommodation, including: (1) to enable objectors to practice medicine without undermining their moral integrity; (2) to respect objectors' autonomy; (3) to promote toleration; (4) to acknowledge epistemic humility; (5) to promote moral progress; (6) to promote quality patient care; (7) to promote diversity in the medical profession; and (8) to avoid discouraging ethically sensitive persons from entering and remaining in the medical profession.

There are also several arguments against accommodation. One type of argument maintains that refusing to provide medical services that are legal, standard of care, and within the scope of a physician's clinical competency is contrary to their professional obligations (incompatibilism). There are two versions of incompatibilism. One argues that conscientious refusals are incompatible with the scope of professional practice. The other maintains that conscientious refusals are contrary to physicians' fiduciary obligations and a widely acknowledged principle that they have a professional obligation to put patients' interests or well-being above their own self-interest – the PIFP. None of the arguments considered in this Element offer convincing reasons for incompatibilism – in part due to a failure to provide and justify unambiguous specifications of the scope of professional practice, physicians' fiduciary obligations, or the PIFP.

Nevertheless, physicians' obligations to their patients impose legitimate constraints on accommodation, and doctors also have obligations to the public that can justify constraints. Additional constraints on accommodation are justified to prevent discrimination and the imposition of excessive burdens on other health professionals and institutions. Compatibilists can maintain that constraints ensure that accommodation does not permit refusals that are contrary to physicians' professional obligations.

Although some compatibilists endorse requirements to disclose information and refer to willing providers, the justification for these unconditional requirements is questionable. There is an alternative that accommodates physicians who have complicity-based objections – disclosing information and referral are required unless there is good reason to believe they are not needed to protect patients' timely access to the medical services at issue. This requirement is outcome-focused rather than act-focused.

Some compatibilists endorse a reason-giving requirement – one that requires objectors to offer a public justification. Some endorse it to reduce the number of refusals and protect patient access. Some have endorsed a sliding-scale criterion of stringency to assess justifications – more or less demanding depending on what is needed in the circumstances to protect access. However, a more direct and transparent approach is a set of constraints specifically designed to ensure that accommodation will not unjustifiably impede patient access.

In the absence of unambiguous, justifiable criteria for evaluating justifications, assessing them can be unduly influenced by subjectivity and biases – which risks thwarting the aim of providing moral space in which objectors can practice medicine without undermining their own moral beliefs. In addition, some objectors may lack the analytic skills required to provide a satisfactory justification; or, even if they possess those skills, they may not want to publicly disclose beliefs that they consider to be intimate and private.

There is substantial asymmetry in law and public and institutional policy between the response to conscientious objection and provision. Whereas conscientious objectors often receive (conditional) accommodation, physicians who believe they have an obligation to provide prohibited services typically are not accommodated. Several attempts to justify this asymmetry are unpersuasive. However, one justification is not easily refuted: the claim that whereas accommodating conscientious objectors does not necessarily thwart the aim of making all standard-of-care medical services available to patients, accommodating conscientious providers thwarts the aim of prohibiting specific medical services. One response is to offer partial accommodation to conscientious providers by reducing the sanctions and penalties they would otherwise face. A second response is to question whether it is justified to thwart access to the medical services at issue.

There are several unresolved issues and ongoing controversies that suggest directions for future scholarship. These include the following:

Professional obligations: Resolving ongoing debates between compatibilists and incompatibilists requires a justified specification of physicians' obligations that can provide unambiguous criteria for determining whether conscientious refusals are contrary to physicians' obligations. Justified, unambiguous criteria are also needed to ascertain when harms and burdens to patients and third parties are *excessive*.

Institutional approaches: Is an institutional approach that places the primary responsibility of protecting access on the profession rather than on individual physicians practicable? Can it adequately protect patients? To what extent are the specific features and practicability of an institutional approach dependent on a society's legal and political institutions, health-care system, socioeconomic conditions, and cultural norms? Might it be possible to design and implement pilot or demonstration projects?

Complicity-based refusals: Resolving persistent debates about whether to accommodate complicity-based refusals – for example, refusals to disclose or refer – requires (1) a justifiable conception of complicity and (2) justified, unambiguous criteria for distinguishing between complicity-based claims of conscience that establish legitimate claims for accommodation and those that do not.

Moral integrity: Which conception of moral integrity, if any, provides a basis for legitimate claims that providing a medical service undermines a physician's moral integrity? Is there more than one such conception?

Core moral beliefs: What are their distinguishing characteristics? Are they "epistemically opaque?"

Reason-giving: Answers to questions that can contribute to a resolution of continuing debates about reason-giving include the following: (1) Other than for the legitimate aims of identifying objections based on discriminatory beliefs or beliefs that are demonstrably false or incompatible with core goals of medicine, is a reason-giving requirement justified? (2) Are there justifiable criteria for evaluating objectors' reasons that are unambiguous and that can prevent excessively subjective and biased reviews? (3) Who or what entity should conduct reviews – department chairs, ethics committees, licensing boards, or special tribunals? (4) What procedural rules, if any, are needed to ensure fairness and protect objectors?

Constraints: Are unconditional act-focused constraints such as requirements to disclose and refer justified? Is a better alternative outcome-focused require-ments – for example, requirements that consider whether disclosure or referral by an objector is essential in the specific circumstances?

Empirical claims: Many arguments by critics and proponents of conscien-tious objection include factual claims. More empirical research will help assess these claims and reduce reliance on speculation. Examples include claims about harms and burdens, trust, the consequences of refusals, the consequences of not tolerating conscientious refusals, the subjective impact of refusals on patients, and the likelihood of insincere objections.

Enforcement mechanisms: What enforcement mechanisms, if any, are needed to ensure compliance with ethical guidelines?

Conscientious provision: Compared to conscientious objection, there is relatively little scholarly literature on conscientious provision. This makes it an especially fertile area for future scholarship.

Notes

1. Sibley and Jacob 1952.
2. Wicclair 2014a.
3. Skorupski 2010; Wicclair 2013.
4. Butler 1983.
5. Lawrence and Curlin 2007.
6. Langston 2001.
7. Nussbaum 2008.
8. Kant 1991, 1997; Hill 1998; Wood 2008.
9. Kant 1997.
10. Childress 1979.
11. Childress 1979, 320.
12. Fuss 1964; D'Arcy 1977.
13. Freud 1962, 70–71.
14. Nussbaum 2008, 19.
15. Nussbaum 2008, 37.
16. Bayles 1979, 167.
17. Chervenak and McCullough 2008.
18. Chervenak and McCullough 2008, 232e2.
19. Stein 2005, 1.
20. Sulmasy 2008.
21. Sulmasy 2008, 141.
22. Brownlee 2012.
23. Childress 1985.
24. Harris 2012.
25. Dickens and Cook 2011.
26. Paris 2023.
27. Guttmacher Institute 2023.
28. Wicclair 2011.
29. Cox, La, and Levine 2013.
30. Williams 1973.
31. Bigelow and Pargettre 2007.
32. Calhoun 1995.
33. Ashford 2000.
34. McFall 1987.
35. Halfon 1989.
36. McFall 1987.
37. McFall 1987, 12.
38. McFall 1987, 13.
39. Wicclair 2011.
40. Hepler 2005, 434.
41. White and Brody 2011, 1805.
42. Blustein 1993, 290.

43. Card 2020.
44. Calhoun 1995.
45. Ashford 2000, 424.
46. McFall 1987, 11.
47. Giubilini 2014.
48. Byrnes 2021.
49. Byrnes 2021, 298.
50. Wicclair 2021.
51. Byrnes 2021, 299.
52. Byrnes 2021, 300.
53. Byrnes 2021, 300.
54. Byrnes 2021, 303.
55. Meyers and Woods 2007.
56. Beauchamp and Childress 2019, 104.
57. McLeod 2020b.
58. Wear, LaGaipa, and Logue 1994, 147.
59. Sulmasy 2019, 507.
60. Sulmasy 2008.
61. Kim and Ferguson 2021.
62. White and Brody 2011.
63. Rentmeester 2008.
64. Rentmeester 2008, 27.
65. White and Brody 2011.
66. Glasber, Eriksson, and Norberg 2007.
67. White and Brody 2011.
68. White and Brody 2011.
69. Giubilini 2017.
70. Giubilini 2017, 406.
71. Giubilini 2017, 406.
72. Rhodes 2006.
73. Stahl and Emanuel 2017, 1383.
74. Giubilini 2017, 404.
75. Giubilini 2017, 407.
76. Schuklenk and Smalling 2017; Stahl and Emanuel 2017.
77. Stahl and Emanuel 2017.
78. Schuklenk and Smalling 2017, 234.
79. Schuklenk and Smalling 2017, 238.
80. Schuklenk and Smalling 2017, 239.
81. Fernandez Lynch 2008, 180.
82. Rhodes 2006; Savulescu and Schuklenk 2017; Schuklenk and Smalling 2017.
83. Schuklenk and Smalling 2017, 238.
84. Robinson 2021, 4
85. AMA CEJA 2017.
86. General Medical Council 2024.
87. McLeod 2020b.

88. McLeod 2020b, 126.
89. Pellegrino 2001.
90. Rhodes 2006.
91. Rhodes 2020.
92. Wicclair 2011a.
93. Giubilini 2017; Savulescu and Schuklenk 2017; Schuklenk and Smalling 2017; Stahl and Emanuel 2017.
94. Stahl and Emanuel 2017.
95. Stahl and Emanuel 2017, 1381.
96. Schuklenk and Smalling 2017, 238.
97. Rhodes 2006, 78.
98. Rhodes 2020, 335.
99. Smalling and Schuklenk 2017, 254.
100. Smalling and Schuklenk 2017, 256.
101. Fernandez Lynch 2008, 99.
102. McLeod 2020b.
103. McLeod 2020b, 52.
104. McLeod 2020b, 52–53.
105. McLeod 2020b, 53.
106. McLeod 2020b, 54.
107. Feinberg 1984.
108. McLeod 2020b, 55.
109. McLeod 2020b, 56.
110. McLeod 2020b, 13.
111. Little and Lyerly 2013, 261.
112. Little and Lyerly 2013, 261.
113. McLeod 2020b, 53.
114. Buetow and Gauld 2018.
115. McLeod 2020b, 75.
116. Gomez 2022.
117. McLeod 2020b, 2.
118. McLeod 2020b, 139–40.
119. McLeod 2020b, 65.
120. McLeod 2002, 2020a.
121. Baier 1986.
122. McLeod 2020b, 68.
123. McLeod 2020b, 68.
124. McLeod 2020b, 71.
125. McLeod 2020b, 71.
126. McLeod 2020b, 72.
127. McLeod 2020b, 73.
128. McLeod 2020b, 75.
129. McLeod 2020b, 76.
130. McLeod 2020b, 77.
131. McLeod 2020b, 87.
132. McLeod 2020b, 78–79.

133. McLeod 2020b, 163.
134. McLeod 2020b, 177.
135. McLeod 2020b, 166–67.
136. McLeod 2020b, 175.
137. McLeod 2020b, 175.
138. McLeod 2020b, 175.
139. Giubilini 2020.
140. Wicclair 2014b.
141. Wicclair 2014b.
142. Schuklenk and Smalling 2017, 238.
143. Meyers and Woods 1996, 119.
144. Card 2020.
145. Meyers and Woods 1996, 120.
146. Fernandez Lynch 2008.
147. Savulescu 2006, 297.
148. Schneider and Levin 1999.
149. AMA CEJA 2007.
150. Schuklenk and Smalling 2017.
151. Schuklenk and Smalling 2017, 234.
152. Schuklenk and Smalling 2017, 236.
153. Schuklenk and Smalling 2017, 238.
154. Schuklenk and Smalling 2017, 236.
155. Curlin and Tollefsen 2021.
156. Pellegrino 2001.
157. Miller and Brody 2001.
158. Arras 2001.
159. Veatch 2001.
160. Rhodes 2006, 2020; Daniels 2008; Wicclair 2011.
161. Curlin and Tollefsen 2021, 2.
162. Boorse 2011.
163. Curlin and Tollefsen 2021, 31.
164. Curlin and Tollefsen 2021, 31.
165. Brock 2008.
166. McLeod 2020b.
167. Forrow, Arnold, and Parker 1993.
168. Cowley 2017; Savulescu and Schuklenk 2017; McLeod 2020b.
169. Savulescu and Schuklenk 2017, 168.
170. McLeod 2020b.
171. Cowley 2016b, 2017.
172. Wicclair 2011.
173. Fernandez Lynch 2008.
174. Fernandez Lynch 2008, 192.
175. Fernandez Lynch 2008, 137.
176. Fernandez Lynch 2008, 165.
177. Fernandez Lynch 2008, 165.
178. Fernandez Lynch 2008, 182.

179. Fernandez Lynch 2008, 184.
180. Fernandez Lynch 2008, 184.
181. Fernandez Lynch 2008, 11.
182. Fernandez Lynch 2008, 12.
183. Fernandez Lynch 2008, 197, 214.
184. Meyers and Woods 1996, 2007.
185. Meyers and Woods 1996, 2007.
186. Kantymir and McLeod 2014, 21.
187. Brownlee 2012, 29.
188. Brownlee 2012, 30.
189. Brownlee 2012, 7.
190. Cowley 2016a.
191. Brownlee 2012, 5–7.
192. Meyers and Woods 1996.
193. Cowley 2016a, 70.
194. Card 2020.
195. Card 2020, 77.
196. Card 2020, 76.
197. Fernandez Lynch 2008, 236.
198. Fernandez Lynch 2008, 237.
199. Fernandez Lynch 2008, 237.
200. Fernandez Lynch 2008, 238.
201. Fernandez Lynch 2008, 238.
202. Fernandez Lynch 2008, 238.
203. Magelssen 2012.
204. Magelssen 2012, 20.
205. Magelssen 2012, 20.
206. Magelssen 2012, 20.
207. Magelssen 2012, 20.
208. Card 2007.
209. Card 2007, 11.
210. Card 2007, 11.
211. Card 2007, 12.
212. Card 2007, 12.
213. Marsh 2014.
214. Marsh 2014, 319.
215. Hughes 2017.
216. Hughes 2017, 216.
217. Card 2014, 320.
218. Card 2014, 321.
219. Card 2014, 323.
220. Card 2020.
221. Card 2017a.
222. Card 2017b, 2020.
223. Card 2020, 21.
224. Card 2020, 21.

225. Card 2020, 22.
226. Ben-Moshe 2019, 406.
227. Card 2020, 93.
228. Ben-Moshe 2021.
229. Ben-Moshe 2021, 285.
230. Ben-Moshe 2021, 285.
231. McConnell and Card 2019.
232. McConnell and Card 2019, 625.
233. Ben-Moshe 2019, 408.
234. Ben-Moshe 2019, 404.
235. Ben-Moshe 2019, 408.
236. Ben-Moshe 2019, 409.
237. Ben-Moshe 2019, 409.
238. Clarke 2019; Saad 2019.
239. Sepper 2012; Fritz 2021; Fox 2023.
240. Fritz 2021.
241. Fritz 2021.
242. Wicclair 2009.
243. Fox 2023.
244. Brummett 2020.
245. Wicclair 2009; Fritz 2021; Fox 2023.
246. Singer 1965, 98–99.
247. Narveson 1985, 51.
248. Malm 1991, 187.
249. Belliotti 1981, 82.
250. Davis 1980, 179.
251. Fritz 2021; Fox 2023.
252. Joffe 1995.
253. Harris 2012, 982.
254. Fernandez Lynch and Stahl 2018.
255. Fox 2023, 1064–65.
256. Fox 2023, 1067.
257. Fox 2023, 1065.
258. Brummett 2020.
259. Brummett 2020, 139.
260. Brummett 2020, 140.
261. Wilkinson 2020.
262. Giubilini 2020, 151.
263. Fritz 2021.
264. Fritz 2021; McLeod 2021.
265. Giubilini 2020.
266. Wicclair 2014b.
267. Fritz 2021.
268. Fox 2023, 1077.
269. Wilkinson 2020.
270. Durland 2011.

271. Annas 1987, 21.
272. Wicclair 2011.
273. Wildes 1997, 416.
274. Committee on Doctrine of the United States Conference of Catholic Bishops 2018.
275. Wicclair 2011.
276. Wicclair 2009; Fritz 2021.
277. Wicclair 2009; Fritz 2021.
278. Fritz 2021; Fox 2023.
279. Minerva 2015.
280. Fox 2023, 1074.
281. Fox 2023.
282. Sepper 2012; Fox 2023.
283. Fox 2023, 1087.
284. Fox 2023, 1087.
285. Fox 2023, 1087.
286. Fox 2023.

References

American Medical Association Council on Ethical and Judicial Affairs [AMA CEJA]. Modification of Ethics Policy to Ensure Inclusion for Transgender Physicians, Medical Students, and Patients. Report of the Council on Ethical and Judicial Affairs, CEJA Report 2-I-07, 2007. https://bit.ly/3Os5G56.

Code of Medical Ethics. Chicago, IL: American Medical Association, 2017.

Annas, George J. Transferring the Ethical Hot Potato. *Hastings Center Report* 17 (1987): 20–21.

Arras, John D. A Method in Search of a Purpose: The Internal Morality of Medicine. *Journal of Medicine and Philosophy* 26 (2001): 643–62.

Ashford, Elizabeth. Utilitarianism, Integrity, and Partiality. *Journal of Philosophy* 97 (2000): 421–39.

Baier, Annette. Trust and Antitrust. *Ethics* 96 (1986): 231–60.

Bayles, Michael D. A Problem of Clean Hands: Refusal to Provide Professional Services. *Social Theory and Practice* 5 (1979): 165–81.

Beauchamp, Tom L., and James F. Childress. *Principles of Biomedical Ethics.* Eighth ed. New York: Oxford University Press, 2019.

Belliotti, Raymond A. Negative and Positive Duties. *Theoria* 47 (1981): 82–92.

Ben-Moshe, Nir. The Truth Behind Conscientious Objection in Medicine. *Journal of Medical Ethics* 45 (2019): 404–10.

Conscientious Objection in Medicine: Making It Public. *HEC Forum* 33 (2021): 269–89.

Bigelow, John, and Robert Pargettre. Integrity and Autonomy. *American Philosophical Quarterly* 44 (2007): 39–49.

Blustein, Jeffrey. Doing What the Patient Orders: Maintaining Integrity in the Doctor–Patient Relationship. *Bioethics* 7 (1993): 289–314.

Boorse, Christopher. Concepts of Health and Disease. In *Handbook of the Philosophy of Science*, edited by Fred Gifford, 13–64. Oxford: Elsevier, 2011.

Brock, Dan. Conscientious Refusal by Physicians and Pharmacists: Who Is Obligated to Do What, and Why? *Theoretical Medicine and Bioethics* 29 (2008): 187–200.

Brownlee, Kimberley. *Conscience and Conviction: The Case for Civil Disobedience.* Oxford: Oxford University Press, 2012.

Brummett, Abram L. Should Positive Claims of Conscience Receive the Same Protection As Negative Claims of Conscience? Clarifying the Asymmetry Debate. *Journal of Clinical Ethics* 31 (2020): 136–42.

Buetow, Stephen, and Natalie Gauld. Conscientious Objection and Person-Centered Care. *Theoretical Medicine and Bioethics* 39 (2018): 143–55.

Butler, Joseph. *Five Sermons Preached at the Rolls Chapel and a Dissertation upon the Nature of Virtue.* Indianapolis, IN: Hackett Publishing Company, 1983.

Byrnes, Jeffrey. The Problem of "Core Moral Beliefs" as the Ground of Conscientious Objection. *HEC Forum* 33 (2021): 291–305.

Calhoun, Cheshire. Standing for Something. *Journal of Philosophy* 92 (1995): 235–60.

Card, Robert F. Conscientious Objection and Emergency Contraception. *American Journal of Bioethics* 7 (2007): 8–14.

Conscientious Objection, Emergency Contraception, and Public Policy. *Journal of Medicine and Philosophy* 36 (2011): 53–58.

Reasonability and Conscientious Objection in Medicine: A Reply to Marsh and an Elaboration of the Reason-Giving Requirement. *Bioethics* 28 (2014): 320–26.

In Defence of Medical Tribunals and the Reasonability Standard for Conscientious Objection in Medicine. *Journal of Medical Ethics* 42 (2016): 73–75.

Reasons, Reasonability and Establishing Conscientious Objector Status in Medicine. *Journal of Medical Ethics* 43 (2017a): 222–25.

The Inevitability of Assessing Reasons in Debates about Conscientious Objection in Medicine. *Cambridge Quarterly of Healthcare Ethics* 26 (2017b): 82–96.

A New Theory of Conscientious Objection in Medicine: Justification and Reasonability. New York: Routledge, 2020.

Chervenak, Frank A., and Laurence B. McCullough. The Ethics of Direct and Indirect Referral for Termination of Pregnancy. *American Journal of Obstetrics and Gynecology* 199 (2008): 232e1–32e3.

Childress, James F. Appeals to Conscience. *Ethics* 89 (1979): 315–35.

Civil Disobedience, Conscientious Objection, and Evasive Noncompliance: A Framework for the Analysis and Assessment of Illegal Actions in Health Care. *Journal of Medicine and Philosophy* 10 (1985): 63–83.

Clarke, Steve. Some Difficulties Involved in Locating the Truth behind Conscientious Objection in Medicine. *Journal of Medical Ethics* 45 (2019): 679–80.

Committee on Doctrine of the United States Conference of Catholic Bishops. Ethical and Religious Directives for Catholic Health Care Services. 6th edition, 2018. https://bit.ly/42uz6VU.

Cowley, Christopher. Conscientious Objection and Healthcare in the UK: Why Tribunals Are Not the Answer. *Journal of Medical Ethics* 42 (2016a): 69–72.

A Defence of Conscientious Objection in Medicine: A Reply to Schuklenk and Savulescu. *Bioethics* 30 (2016b): 358–64.

Conscientious Objection in Healthcare and the Duty to Refer. *Journal of Medical Ethics* 43 (2017): 207–12.

Cox, Damian, Marguerite La Caze, and Michael Levine. Integrity. In *The Stanford Encyclopedia of Philosophy*, edited by Edward N. Zalta, 2013. https://plato.stanford.edu/entries/integrity/.

Curlin, Farr, and Christopher Tollefsen. *The Way of Medicine: Ethics and the Healing Profession.* Notre Dame, IN: University of Notre Dame Press, 2021.

D'Arcy, Eric. Conscience. *Journal of Medical Ethics* 3 (1977): 98–99.

Daniels, Norman. *Just Health: Meeting Health Needs Fairly.* Cambridge: Cambridge University Press, 2008.

Davis, Nancy. The Priority of Avoiding Harm. In *Killing and Letting Die*, edited by Bonnie Steinbock, 172–214. Englewood Cliffs, NJ: Prentice-Hall, 1980.

Dickens, Bernard M., and Rebecca J. Cook. Conscientious Commitment to Women's Health. *International Journal of Gynecology & Obstetrics* 113 (2011): 163–66.

Durland, Spencer L. The Case against Institutional Conscience. *Notre Dame Law Review* 86 (2011): 1655–86.

Feinberg, Joel. *The Moral Limits of the Criminal Law: Harm to Others.* Vol. 1. New York: Oxford University Press, 1984.

Fernandez Lynch, Holly. *Conflicts of Conscience in Health Care: An Institutional Compromise.* Cambridge, MA: The MIT Press, 2008.

Fernandez Lynch, Holly, and Ronit Y. Stahl. Opinion, Protecting Conscientious Providers of Health Care. *New York Times*, January 26, 2018.

Forrow, Lachlan, Robert M. Arnold, and Lisa S. Parker. Preventive Ethics: Expanding the Horizons of Clinical Ethics. *Journal of Clinical Ethics* 4 (1993): 287–94.

Fox, Dov. Medical Disobedience. *Harvard Law Review* 136 (2023): 1030–111.

Freud, Sigmund. *Civilization and Its Discontents.* Translated by James Strachey. New York: W. W. Norton & Co., 1962.

Fritz, Kyle. Unjustified Asymmetry: Positive Claims of Conscience and Heartbeat Bills. *American Journal of Bioethics* 21 (2021): 46–59.

Fuss, Peter. Conscience. *Ethics* 74 (1964): 111–20.

General Medical Council. Good Medical Practice, 2024. www.gmc-uk.org/-/media/documents/gmp-2024-final—english_pdf-102607294.pdf.

Giubilini, Alberto. The Paradox of Conscientious Objection and the Anemic Concept of "Conscience": Downplaying the Role of Moral Integrity in Health Care. *Kennedy Institute of Ethics Journal* 24 (2014): 159–85.

Objection to Conscience: An Argument against Conscience Exemptions in Healthcare. *Bioethics* 31 (2017): 400–08.

Conscientious Objection in Healthcare: Neither a Negative nor a Positive Right. *Journal of Clinical Ethics* 31 (2020): 146–53.

Glasber, A. L., S. Eriksson, and A. Norberg. Burnout and "Stress of Conscience" among Healthcare Personnel. *Journal of Advanced Nursing* 57 (2007): 392–403.

Gomez, Javiera Perez. Mcleod's Conscience in Reproductive Health Care: Fiduciary Duties beyond Reproductive Care, the Role of the Pharmacist, and the Harms and Wrongs of Conscientious Refusals. *International Journal of Feminist Approaches to Bioethics* 15 (2022): 137–43.

Guttmacher Institute. An Overview of Abortion Laws, August 31, 2023. www.guttmacher.org/state-policy/explore/overview-abortion-laws.

Halfon, Mark S. *Integrity: A Philosophical Inquiry.* Philadelphia, PA: Temple University Press, 1989.

Harris, Lisa H. Recognizing Conscience in Abortion Provision. *New England Journal of Medicine* 367 (2012): 981–83.

Hepler, Charles D. Balancing Pharmacists' Conscientious Objections with Their Duty to Serve. *Journal of the American Pharmacists Association* 45 (2005): 434–36.

Hill, Thomas E. Jr. Four Conceptions of Conscience. In *Integrity and Conscience (Nomos XI)*, edited by Ian Shapiro and Robert Adams, 13–52. New York: New York University Press, 1998.

Hughes, Jonathan A. Conscientious Objection in Healthcare: Why Tribunals Might Be the Answer. *Journal of Medical Ethics* 43 (2017): 213–17.

Joffe, Carole E. *Doctors of Conscience: The Struggle to Provide Abortion Before and After Roe v. Wade.* Boston, MA: Beacon Press, 1995.

Kant, Immanuel. *The Metaphysics of Morals.* Translated by Mary Gregor. Cambridge: Cambridge University Press, 1991.

Lectures on Ethics. Translated by Peter Heath. Cambridge: Cambridge University Press, 1997.

Kantymir, Lori, and Carolyn McLeod. Justification for Conscience Exemptions in Health Care. *Bioethics* 28 (2014): 16–23.

Kim, Eric J., and Kyle Ferguson. Does Medicine Need to Accommodate Positive Conscientious Objections to Morally Self-Correct? *American Journal of Bioethics* 21 (2021): 74–76.

Langston, Douglas C. *Conscience and Other Virtues*. University Park, PA: The Pennsylvia State University Press, 2001.

Lawrence, Ryan E., and Farr A. Curlin. Clash of Definitions: Controversies about Conscience in Medicine. *American Journal of Bioethics* 7 (2007): 10–14.

Little, Margaret, and Anne Drapkin Lyerly. The Limits of Conscientious Refusal: A Duty to Ensure Access. *American Medical Association Journal of Ethics* 15 (2013): 257–62.

Magelssen, M. When Should Conscientious Objection Be Accepted? *Journal of Medical Ethics* 38 (2012): 18–21.

Malm, H. M. Between the Horns of the Negative–Positive Duty Debate. *Philosophical Studies* 61 (1991): 187–210.

Marsh, Jason. Conscientious Refusals and Reason-Giving. *Bioethics* 28 (2014): 313–19.

McConnell, Doug, and Robert F. Card. Public Reason in Justifications of Conscientious Objection in Health Care. *Bioethics* 33 (2019): 625–32.

McFall, Lynne. Integrity. *Ethics* 98 (1987): 5–20.

McLeod, Carolyn. *Self-Trust and Reproductive Autonomy*. Cambridge, MA: MIT Press, 2002.

Trust. In *The Stanford Encyclopedia of Philosophy*, edited by Edward N. Zalta and Uri Nodelman, 2020a. https://plato.stanford.edu/entries/trust/.

Conscience in Reproductive Health Care: Prioritizing Patient Interests. Oxford: Oxford University Press, 2020b.

Justified Asymmetries: Positive and Negative Claims to Conscience in Reproductive Health Care. *American Journal of Bioethics* 21 (2021): 60–62.

Meyers, Christopher, and Robert D Woods. An Obligation to Provide Abortion Services: What Happens When Physicians Refuse? *Journal of Medical Ethics* 22 (1996): 115–20.

Conscientious Objection? Yes, but Make Sure It Is Genuine. *American Journal of Bioethics* 7 (2007): 19–20.

Miller, Franklin G., and Howard Brody. The Internal Morality of Medicine: An Evolutionary Perspective. *Journal of Medicine and Philosophy* 26 (2001): 581–99.

Minerva, Francesca. Conscientious Objection in Italy. *Journal of Medical Ethics* 41 (2015): 170–73.

Narveson, Jan. Positive/Negative: Why Bother? *Tulane Studies in Philosophy* XXXIII (1985): 51–65.

Nussbaum, Martha C. *Liberty of Conscience: In Defense of America's Tradition of Religious Equality.* New York: Basic Books, 2008.

Paris, Francesca. Bans on Transition Care for Young People Spread across U.S. *New York Times*, April 17, 2023.

Pellegrino, Edmund D. The Internal Morality of Clinical Medicine: A Paradigm for the Ethics of the Helping and Healing Professions. *Journal of Medicine and Philosophy* 26 (2001): 559–79.

Rentmeester, Christy A. Moral Damage to Health Care Professionals and Trainees: Legalism and Other Consequences for Patients and Colleagues. *Journal of Medicine and Philosophy* 33 (2008): 27–43.

Rhodes, Rosamond. The Ethical Standard of Care. *American Journal of Bioethics* 6 (2006): 76–78.

   The Truted Doctor: Medical Ethics and Professionalism. New York: Oxford University Press, 2020.

Robinson, Michael. Voluntarily Chosen Roles and Conscientious Objection in Health Care. *Journal of Medical Ethics* 48 (2022): 718–22.

Saad, Toni C. Conscientious Objection: Unmasking the Impartial Spectator. *Journal of Medical Ethics* 45 (2019): 676–77.

Savulescu, Julian. Conscientious Objection in Medicine. *British Medical Journal* 332 (2006): 294–97.

Savulescu, Julian, and Udo Schuklenk. Doctors Have No Right to Refuse Medical Assistance in Dying, Abortion, or Contraception. *Bioethics* 31 (2017): 162–70.

Schneider, Jason S., and Saul Levin. Uneasy Partners: The Lesbian and Gay Health Care Community and the AMA. *Journal of the American Medical Association* 282 (1999): 1287–88.

Schuklenk, Udo, and Ricardo Smalling. Why Medical Professionals Have No Moral Claim to Conscientious Objection Accommodation in Liberal Democracies. *Journal of Medical Ethics* 43 (2017): 234–40.

Sepper, Elizabeth. Taking Conscience Seriously. *Virginia Law Review* 98 (2012): 1501–75.

Sibley, Muford Q., and Philip E. Jacob. *Conscription of Conscience: The American State and the Conscientious Objector, 1940–1947.* Ithaca, NY: Cornell University Press, 1952.

Singer, Marcus G. Negative and Positive Duties. *Philosophical Quarterly* 15 (1965): 97–103.

Skorupski, John. Conscience. In *The Routledge Companion to Ethics*, edited by John Skorupski, 550–61. London: Routledge, 2010.

Smalling, Ricardo, and Udo Schuklenk. Against the Accommodation of Subjective Healthcare Provider Beliefs in Medicine: Counteracting Supporters of Conscientious Objector Accommodation Arguments. *Journal of Medical Ethics* 43 (2017): 253–56.

Stahl, Ronit Y., and Ezekiel J. Emanuel. Physicians, Not Conscripts – Conscientious Objection in Health Care. *New England Journal of Medicine* 376 (2017): 1380–85.

Stein, Rob. Pharmacists' Rights at Front of New Debate: Because of Beliefs, Some Refuse to Fill Birth Control Prescriptions. *Washington Post*, March 28, 2005, 1.

Sulmasy, Daniel P. What Is Conscience and Why Is Respect for It So Important? *Theoretical Medicine and Bioethics* 29 (2008): 135–49.

Conscience, Tolerance, and Pluralism in Health Care. *Theoretical Medicine and Bioethics* 40 (2019): 507–21.

Veatch, Robert M. The Impossibility of a Morality Internal to Medicine. *Journal of Medicine and Philosophy* 26 (2001): 621–42.

Wear, Stephen, Susan LaGaipa, and Gerald Logue. Toleration of Moral Diversity and the Conscientious Refusal by Physicians to Withdraw Life-Sustaining Treatments. *Journal of Medicine and Philosophy* 19 (1994): 147–59.

White, Douglas B., and Baruch Brody. Would Accommodating Some Conscientious Objections by Physicians Promote Quality in Medical Care? *Journal of the American Medical Association* 305 (2011): 1804–05.

Wicclair, Mark. Negative and Positive Claims of Conscience. *Cambridge Quarterly of Healthcare Ethics* 18 (2009): 14–22.

Conscientious Objection in Health Care: An Ethical Analysis. Cambridge: Cambridge University Press, 2011a.

Conscientious Refusals by Hospitals and Emergency Contraception. *Cambridge Quarterly of Healthcare Ethics* 20 (2011b): 130–38.

Conscience. In *International Encyclopedia of Ethics*, edited by Hugh LaFollette. Hoboken, NJ: John Wiley & Sons, 2013. https://doi .org/10.1002/9781444367072.wbiee758.

Conscientious Objection. In *Encyclopedia of Global Bioethics*, edited by Henk ten Have, 729–40. Cham: Springer, 2014a.

Managing Conscientious Objection in Health Care Institutions. *HEC Forum* 26 (2014b): 267–83.

Commentary: Special Issue on Conscientious Objection. *HEC Forum* 33 (2021): 307–24.

Wildes, Kevin Wm. Institutional Identity, Integrity, and Conscience. *Kennedy Institute of Ethics Journal* 7 (1997): 413–19.

Wilkinson, Dominic J. C. Positive or Negative? Consistency and Inconsistency in Claims of Conscience. *Journal of Clinical Ethics* 31 (2020): 143–45.

Williams, Bernard. Integrity. In *Utilitarianism: For and Against*, edited by J. J. C Smart and Bernard Williams, 108–17. New York: Cambridge University Press, 1973.

Wood, Allen W. *Kantian Ethics*. Cambridge: Cambridge University Press, 2008.

Cambridge Elements ☰

Bioethics and Neuroethics

Thomasine Kushner

California Pacific Medical Center, San Francisco

Thomasine Kushner, PhD, is the founding Editor of the *Cambridge Quarterly of Healthcare Ethics* and coordinates the International Bioethics Retreat, where bioethicists share their current research projects, the Cambridge Consortium for Bioethics Education, a growing network of global bioethics educators, and the Cambridge-ICM Neuroethics Network, which provides a setting for leading brain scientists and ethicists to learn from each other.

About the Series

Bioethics and neuroethics play pivotal roles in today's debates in philosophy, science, law, and health policy. With the rapid growth of scientific and technological advances, their importance will only increase. This series provides focused and comprehensive coverage in both disciplines consisting of foundational topics, current subjects under discussion and views toward future developments.

Cambridge Elements ⁼

Bioethics and Neuroethics

Printed in the United States
by Baker & Taylor Publisher Services